SELL YOUR WAY TO SUCCESS ON SHOPIFY

How to Create Your Store, Showcase Your Products, and Increase Your Sales
(with B&W Photos)

Gini Graham Scott, PhD

**Author of 200+ Print, E-Books and Audiobooks
and a Changemakers Publishing Shopify Account**

HOW TO CREATE A SHOPIFY STORE TO SHOWCASE AND SELL ANY PRODUCTS

TABLE OF CONTENTS

INTRODUCTION

After I published over 200 books, people kept telling me I should sell them on Shopify, so they would really stand out as a group with a built in audience to promote and sell the books. All of my books would have more of an identity than just posting them on Amazon or IngramSpark. I would also receive more per book, since I wouldn't be paying a distributor or middleman who would give me a royalty. The goal was not to replace these other outlets, but to supplement them and give my publishing company more identity through a Shopify store.

If setting up a Shopify store is a good fit for your company, the first step is to organize and set-up your store so you are ready to sell. Then, you have to promote it like you market and promote anything you are selling to your target market. In designing your store, keep your target market in mind so you have a look and feel that your audience will relate to.

The next step is to get people into your store using the major promotional vehicles for doing this: from the traditional and social media to working out affiliate relationships with others aiming for your target market. Affiliates can sell and promote your products in return for a meaningful commission (typically 40-70%).

Since my forte is creating the store and working with a marketing and publicity team, I will focus on how to set up your store so you are ready to sell. Then, I will touch briefly on the kind of marketing and promotion considerations to keep in mind. I recommend working with your own marketing team to do this rather than trying to do everything yourself. Thys, the emphasis in this book is on a step-by-step guide to setting up your store, getting ready to sell, and launching it to achieve Shopify success.

As for a detailed discussion of the different marketing and promotion methods -- from promoting your store on Facebook and Instagram to doing guest blogs and media appearance -- I leave that for another book by an author specializing in this subject. The basic steps to selling include these:

1) Decide on the products you want to sell.

2) Find photographs of these products -- your own or from your supplier.

3) List the products for sale in your Shopify store.

4) Set up a system so the customer who makes a purchase can pay you.

5) Work out arrangements to fulfill the order, either by sending the products yourself via shipping or email, or by placing an order with a supplier to send the products to the customer.

And that's it! Now let's begin creating your store to showcase and sell any products. I have included screenshots, some from my Changemakers Publishing store, to guide you through the process.

CHAPTER 1: WHY HAVE A STORE ON SHOPIFY

If you have a line of at least six products to sell or want to add products from others, you can use a Shopify store to build your brand, increase your audience, and make sales. You can sell them using drop shipping, a process where you receive an order and send the customer the product yourself or with the help of an assistant. Or you can use a fulfillment service set-up through your store that makes the shipments for you.

Shopify makes a good case for having a store on its website, which indicates how easy it is to set up your store and arrange for shipping. Here's a brief overview from Shopify on why you should have a store and how easy it is to set up. You can set up a store for any kind of products, including books with a broad market appeal, such as self-help, how-to, popular business, and inspirational books. Shopify even has an integration with Facebook and Google advertising, so once your store is set up, you can advertise it.

How You Can Sell Everywhere -- Both Online and In-Person

The big advantage of Shopify is that you can sell everywhere. While most selling is online, you can use Shopify to take orders when you sell at an in-person venue, such as at a trade show, flea market, or pop-up store. You or your customer can use a mobile device to place orders.

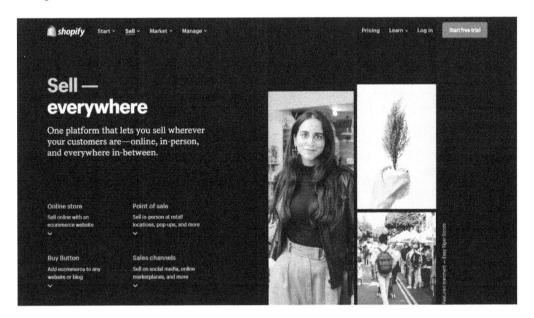

One of the advantages of Shopify is you get a dedicated ecommerce website, which provides templates for building your store, rather than starting from scratch on your own website. You can use various themes to feature your products and list them in various ways -- including best-selling, featured, and by name, listed from A to Z or Z to A. Your shop is then integrated with various systems for shipping and advertising.

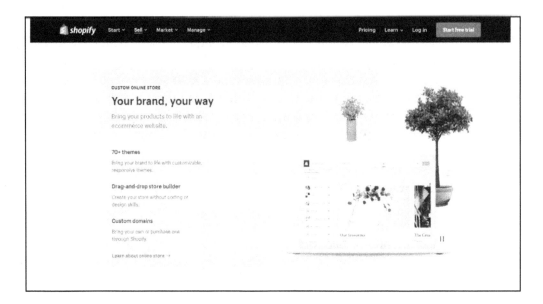

Shopify also offers assorted backend tools to enable you to better manage your inventory and send out mailings about new products or special sales to current or prospective customers.

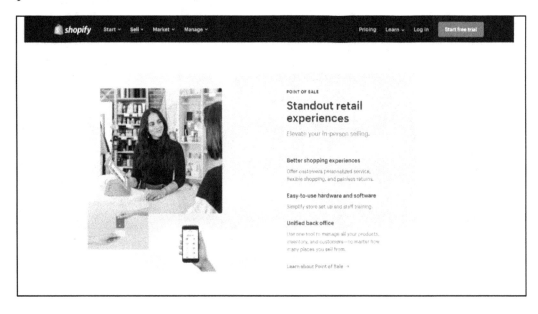

As an alternative to creating your store with Shopify templates, you can integrate a current website or blog into Shopify. This way, if you already have something created, you don't have to create it all over again in Shopify. However, be careful here! If you don't have a well-organized and showcased online store, it may be better to start again, select a template and theme from Shopify, and add your products there.

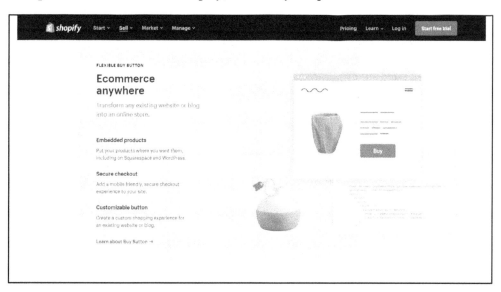

Another advantage of using Shopify rather than your website is you can expand your reach as an ideal complement to selling on Amazon. You can further expand your reach through promotions on the social media. Shopify makes it easy to tap into the biggest online markets and social media places like Facebook and Instagram. You can tap into the power of eBay, too.

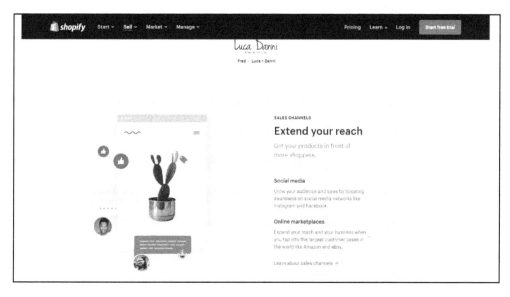

Shopify has various tools to help you find and reach out to your ideal target market. Once you determine your market, Shopify helps you automate reaching out to that audience, and it offers insights on what did well, so you can repeat what works best and modify or stop doing what didn't perform up to standards.

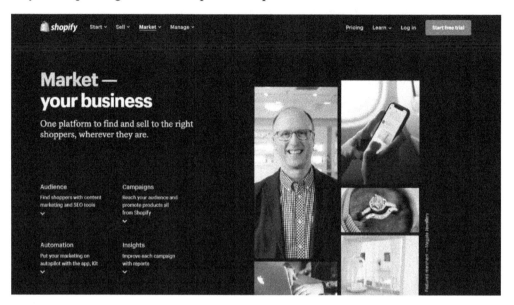

Shopify also provides assistance in connecting with your audience, such as by creating a blog on the platform where you write original content or adapt it from articles you publish elsewhere. It additionally has SEO tools to help you know what keywords to use to help people searching for particular types of products find you.

Another advantage of using Shopify to sell more is that it integrates with the two major advertising platforms -- Google and Facebook. On both platforms, you can target your ad to particular markets based on demographics, interests, and locations.

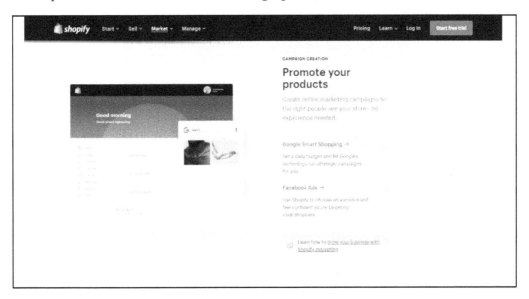

If you don't have the time or interest in doing the marketing or don't have someone to do it for you, Shopify has a virtual marketing assistant to help you drive sales and email customers, called Kit. I didn't use Kit, since I work with a virtual assistant, but check it out for yourself.

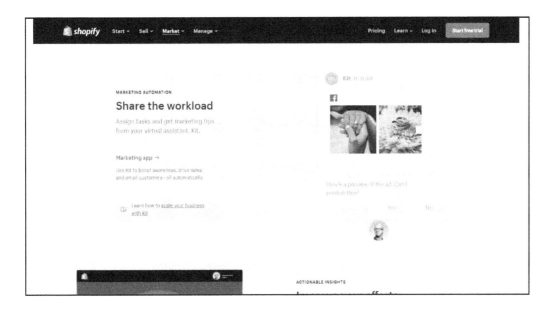

Another tool Shopify offers is marketing research so you can check what is working and what isn't in your campaigns. You can see what is performing well by using the graphs and charts Shopify creates based on your ad campaigns and the number of people responding to your ads.

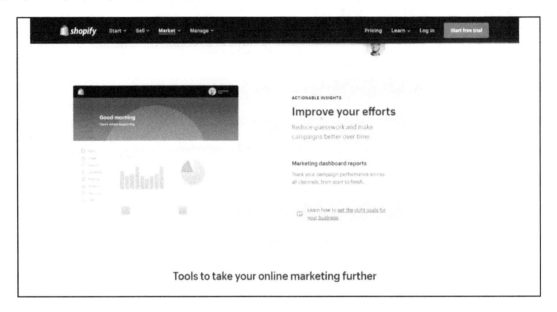

To sum up, the main advantages of creating a Shopify store are these:
1) There are small start-up costs.
2) You have no inventory, since you are selling from photos of your products and you order the products you sell at wholesale.
3) It's low-risk because you invest little in store set-up, don't have to pay in advance for inventory, and after your free trial period, you pay as little as $29 a month.
4) You can offer a wide variety of products, if you supplement your own products with products from other suppliers.
5) Once you set up your store, which takes an hour or two, you can start immediately, since you simply upload the photos of the products you are selling, add a brief description and pricing information.
6) Then, you are ready to start making sales.

CHAPTER 2: DEVELOPING YOUR STORE IDEA

The first step before you set up your Shopify account is deciding what you want to sell. You also need enough products to create a store. These can be your own products, or you can add other sellers' products to the mix, as long as they fit together and are aimed at the same market. If you have multiple products that are targeted to different markets, it may be better to create separate stores.

To get started, target one or related markets, so you aren't scattered. Later, after one store is successful, you can always add another, and then another. So first things first. Start with a single line of products aimed at a selected market.

After you set up your store front, you need to promote it and let people know about it. By targeting your market, you can keep your promotion focused.

Deciding What to Sell

This next consideration could be a no brainer if you already have products in a certain area or have a strong interest in starting a particular type of store. As long as it has a clear market, go for it.

However, there are a few considerations in deciding if this is a good product line to sell. Ask yourself these questions. You should be able to answer yes to each one. If you can't, consider ways to overcome that challenge.

1. **Is this a popular sales category?**
   Some examples might be jewelry, clothing, party supplies, or greeting cards.

2. **Is this a sales category that can be easily sold and shipped online?**
   This should be a product you can easily package and send safely to the buyer. For example, only certain types of food products can be readily shipped, such as candy, cookies, and canned goods. Stay away from anything that involves complicated shipping or products that can easily break on shipment, such as pottery and art pieces. You can certain sell specialty products to certain types of buyers, perhaps through your website, but for a Shopify store, think in terms of popular products that can have large sales and be easily shipped to a buyer.

3. **Is this product line sufficiently different from what others are already selling?**
   You want to give people a reason to buy from you rather than anyone else. While some store owners compete on price, such as selling common products at a lower cost than others, this is usually not a good sales strategy. You will end up

with lower margins and you have to have massive sales to make a profit. Instead, look for something where you can add a unique feature, such as T-shirts with the photos of well-known travel destinations (if someone isn't already doing this) or jewelry, handbags, hats, or other fashionable clothing items designed by you.

4. **Do you have the time and money to market and promote your store?**

It can be great to set up your store with your product line and a beautiful store front to invite buyers to buy. Then, you have to put in the time and effort to get traffic to your store. That usually takes money, such as for ads or for a virtual assistant to do a social media promotion campaign to get buyers to your store. So you need to set up some time to do it yourself or hire someone. Additionally, set up an advertising and promotion budget, such as for ads on Google, Facebook, or YouTube.

If you haven't already run a marketing campaign, consult with a marketing or promotional pro to learn what might be the best strategy for your product line, where to best market it, and what to expect. Then, prepare to test your marketing strategy again and again, because in the beginning, unless you suddenly strike gold, you don't know what approach works the best. You commonly have to do some A and B testing, where you try different approaches that could involve different ad copy, different price points, different products, and different offers until you find what works the best. Then, you can do more of that. The usual guidelines are to start small with a particular ad -- even $5 or $10 for a click through campaign. Then, if an ad performs well, you can increase your budget, say to $20 to $25, see what the results are, and if you ads are having good results, go up to the next level. A marketing consultant can help you plan such an ad campaign. If you aren't marketing savvy yourself, I recommend you work with someone who can help you strategize what to do, so you or someone you hire can implement whatever approach you choose on a day-to-day basis.

5. **Do you want to sell only your own products or do you want to include other product lines?**

If you have enough products of your own, it's great to start with those and it can be very fulfilling to create a shop around your own products. After all, it can be personally satisfying to see that people want to buy what you create.

But if you only have a few self-created products, it's better to launch your store with some related products from others appealing to the same market. In fact, consider becoming partners with one or two other partners in a similar situation with only a few products. Together you might share the time and costs of launching the store. Alternatively, work out an arrangement with others where you promote their products and get a commission or pay a wholesale price for their products. An advantage of an online store is that all you need is a photograph and sales copy for what you are selling, so you don't need extensive inventory, and you can pay for individual items or a small quantity (say 3 to 6 items) to start. Instead of stocking your shelves with inventory, you just need some compelling photos of the items for sale.

6. **Do you have a convenient location where you can organize your business, run your store, and respond to customers yourself or with an employee or virtual assistant?**

You want to think of your Shopify store like operating any business, and you ideally need a dedicated place from which to run it. For example, is there a quiet room in your house where you can set up a computer and files to keep track of sales? It can be fine to keep all of your records online if you prefer that, but I like to print out and have a hard copy as well for backup and because I like to organize product photos and sales copy that way. This way, I can easily look at them as a group, rather than looking at photo files and sales copy one by one on my computer. Use whatever approach works best for you, and have a room or area in a room you can use for running your online retail store as a business.

In some cases, you might set up your Shopify store to sell your products in addition to selling in a physical space, such as a booth in a flea market, a retail store, or an in-home sales party. In this case, you might promote your store in these other venues to give prospective customers a choice of how they want to buy. If you go to business networking events or belong to a local Chamber of Commerce, you might provide flyers about your store to get people to go there and buy. Or if you have a booth at a trade show, you can both sell from your booth or invite people to visit your Shopify store and buy there.

What's the best approach for you? Consider your Shopify store one of many outlets for your products. The particular strategy and product mix is one you can determine by testing yourself or go over with a marketing consultant. As you make decisions about what to sell in your store and how to combine your store with other sales and marketing choices, design your store and sales materials accordingly.

Choosing a Store Name

Once you decide what to sell, come up with a store name. That's the first thing Shopify will ask when you set up your store. This name will also be the center of your branding campaign.

If you already have a name for a retail store, use that. Likewise, if you have a name for your store on your website or Facebook page, use that if you have a following.

But if you are just getting started, choose a name for your store which expresses your brand. Use your name if you are creating a brand around that, such as "Jane Smith Sales" or "Jane Smith Fashion Designs". Otherwise, pick a name that expresses your essence and is catchy and memorable, as long as no one else is using that name. Go on Google to check any name you are considering and see if anyone is using it. For example, if you are going to sell trendy fashions, you might use something like: "Flair Fashions." If you featuring sports equipment, maybe a name like "Sportsorama". If you are selling jewelry, maybe "Gems by Jen" (if that's your name).

Choosing a Domain Name

You can do a search for domain names to see if anyone has the same or a similar name to one you are considering for a website. Check one of the services that sell domains such as Dotster.com, which is the main service I use. Then, go to Search or Register a Domain and put in the name you are considering.

If the name you select is already taken, check who has that domain and if there is a going company there. If not, or if you find a company is simply selling the name, come up with an alternative that conveys the essence of your branding, such as "Flair Fashions House" instead of "Flair Fashions," or "TheSportsorama" instead of "Sportsorama." If the company already using the name is doing something similar, don't use it, because you could run into confusion and lose customers to the other company with a similar name.

Another option if the name is parked somewhere and for sale at a premium price – typically about $500-2500– is to choose a common alternative such as .net, .org, or .info at a regular domain price. If there is no active dot com domain, that could be a good alternative. If you do find a very close domain name to the one you are considering, it may be best to choose a different name and then look for domain names related to that.

Once you select a name, consider different variations on it which you can use for your Shopify store. For instance, if you have a .com name, you might use a .net name for your store. As an example, I have ChangemakersPublishing.com for a subdomain on my website www.changemakerspublishingandwriting.com which features my books. But I use www.changemakerspublishing.net for my Shopify name.

Selecting an Email

Additionally, pick out an email for your Shopify account. It's best to create a different email from your regular email, so if you start getting a volume of email through Shopify, you can separate it from your other email. One option is setting up a separate yahoo.com or gmail.com account. Another option is using an email connected to your domain. Then, if you don't want to go to the website for your email, forward it to whatever other email you set up. For instance, use sales@yourdomainname.com or info@yourdomainname.com. I recommend using "sales," since you can use "info" for general inquiries and "press" or "media" for inquiries from the media.

PART I: SETTING UP YOUR SHOPIFY ACCOUNT

CHAPTER 3: GETTING STARTED ON SHOPIFY

Okay, so you decided on the products you want to sell. The next step is to go to Shopify and open up an account. When you go to the site, a good way to start is with the 14 day trial. Just click "Start Your Free" trial, which appears on the opening pages of the site.

Simply sign in to start your free trial. You will get a sign-up form that asks for your email, password, and your store name.

If you haven't already selected your email and store name, as discussed in Chapter 2, select it now so you can begin setting up your account.

Your sign-up form for 14 days will look something like this.

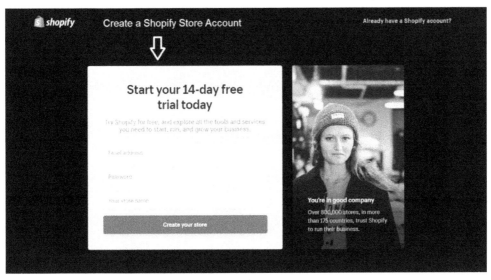

Next, you add in your address, so Shopify can set up your currencies and tax rates, based on your location.

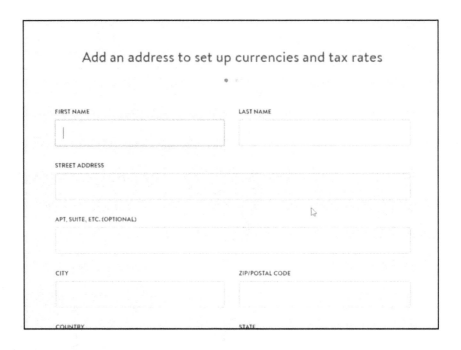

Then, you will be asked to describe whether you are already selling anything, and if so, how much are you earning, or if you are setting up a store for a client.

Once you provide that information, this will create your store and start your 14 day free trial, which is how I began my store. At any point during the trial, you can select a plan, which starts at $29 a month. Meanwhile, you can start setting up your store and discover how Shopify works for you.

You will also get assorted options for how to sell with Shopify, including selling in person where you make point of sales (POS) directly to a customer. Plus you can sell on Facebook or add the products you want to sell on Shopify to an existing website. The invitation to "Install Oberlo" is a way to add products available through the e-commerce Oberlo store. But if you are selling only your own products or want to obtain products from individual distributors or local companies, skip this invitation.

Next you will be asked some questions about your store name, the email for Shopify and customers to contact you, the legal name of your business, and your phone number and address.

Then, you will be given details on your current plan (a trial for the next 14 days, unless you upgrade it) and asked to add your billing information and information on anyone with access to your account. For instance, I had a virtual assistant who set up my account, so I gave her this access.

After that, add in your credit card information, so Shopify can bill you once you transfer to a monthly payment plan.

The basic plan when you start selling is $29 a month. You can later upgrade to another plan when you are ready to expand your sales and use more sales features. The credit card rates are what Shopify charges when someone makes a credit card purchase.

Once you start on this plan, you can pay on a yearly basis, and save $36 a year, though I chose the $29 a month plan. If you pay by the month, you can cancel at any time without losing your unused investment.

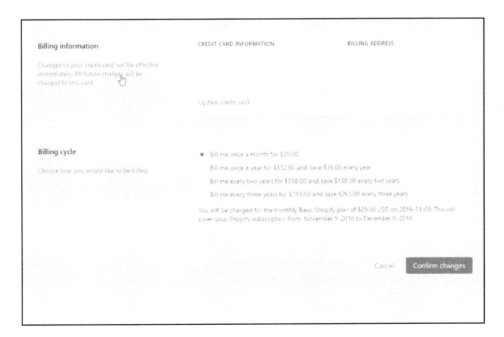

If you already have set up your domain name, you connect your store to that, and you will see it indicated in your account. If you don't yet have a domain name, you can purchase one through Shopify.

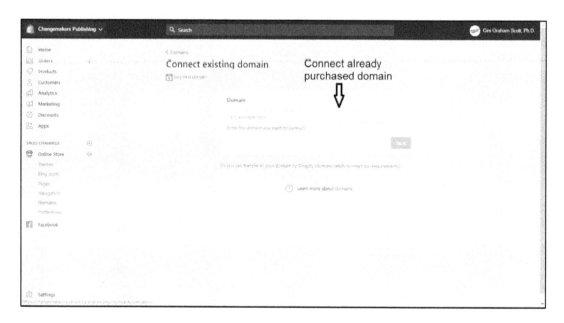

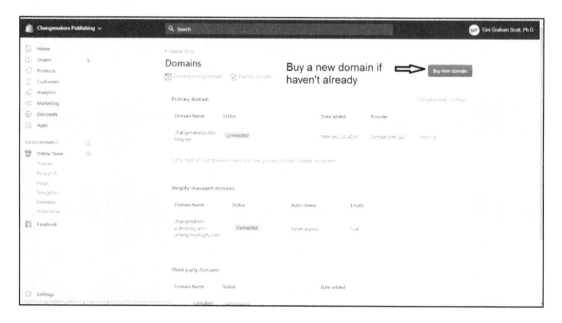

After you set up your store, you can see on a daily basis what's happening with your store.

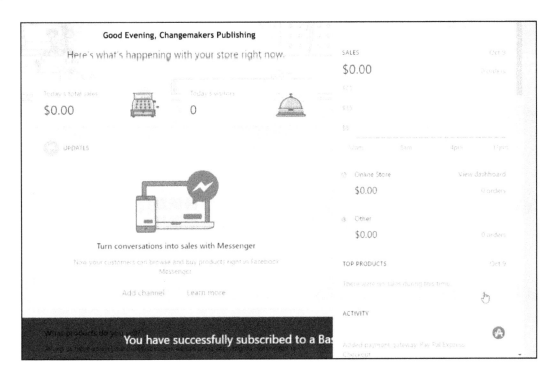

CHAPTER 4: SELLING YOUR OWN PRODUCTS

If you have your own line of products to sell, start with those. You can add products from other sources to supplement your product line if you only have a small number of products. In my case, I have about 150 books, so I started with those.

While you can add our products first and then select a theme, it can help you organize your store if you select your theme first and then select your products.

A good way to think of a theme is like designing and installing the decorations in a retail store -- or upgrading how your store looks after adding your products. I started by setting up my books first. Then, I selected a theme, and my assistant organized my books into a set of collections or types of books. But you can do this in any order: products - collections - themes; themes - products - collections; or products - themes - collections.

Here's one of my product pages before setting up a theme.

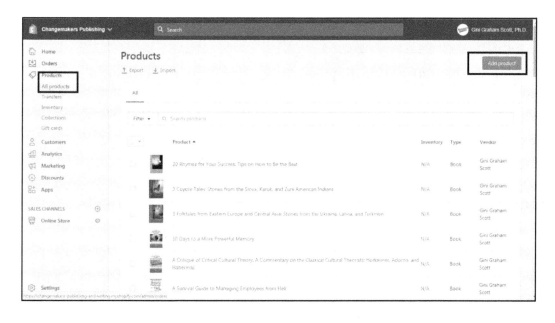

For each product you add, you have to add a title and description. If you buy a product from someone else to sell, the seller will provide that information. Add a product image for each product you sell -- in my case, the cover of each of my books.

You also need to provide the product price, and if you are fulfilling the orders yourself, indicate how many items you have in stock. If you have inventory on hand, use that number. However, if it's a print-on-demand product, such as the print-on-demand books I am publishing, add any reasonable number that you might be able to produce in a short period of time, based on the orders you are likely to get. For instance, I typically say I have one or two dozen copies available both to give prospective buyers a sense of scarcity to get it now and to suggest that this is a reasonably popular item. Indicating only one or two copies available might suggest the book might not be selling well.

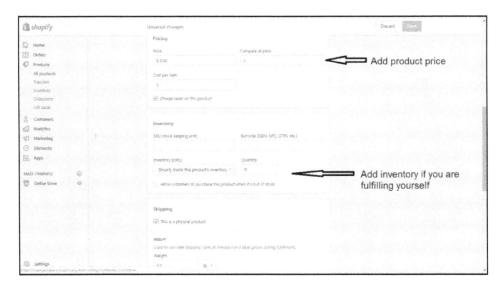

30

Initially, you can upload your products without putting them in collections, though it's a good idea to organize them. Otherwise they are listed all together and customers can find them listed from A-Z, Z-A, the best-selling, and the most recent from first to last or last to first. Later, you can create a section for featured products, too.

Here I'll only describe creating collections briefly. Later, I'll have a chapter on how to organize your products into collections.

The first step is to go to the collections tab on Shopify and click the Create Collection Link.

Next, give your collection a name.

Then, set up the collection type, where you can enter the products into a collection manually or automatically. To enter products automatically, assign a product tag to each product so that all products with the same tag become part of that collection.

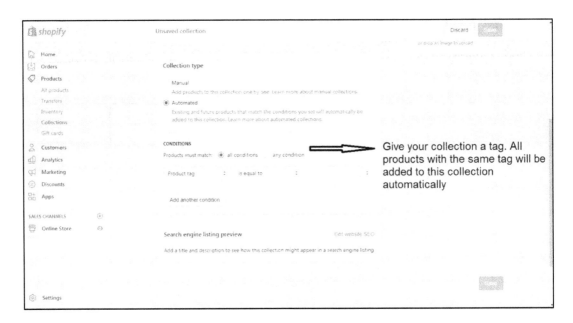

You can similarly use this approach to add products for a business associate. In either case, you need to add shipping arrangements and costs to be discussed in a later chapter.

Now you know the basics about selecting your own products and placing them in your shop. In the next chapter, I'll discuss adding other products with a little help from an app that will enable you to order products from a major supplier.

CHAPTER 5: FIND OTHER PRODUCTS TO SELL

If you are just getting started, you might want to supplement your own products with products from others. If so, you can add their products by including photos and pricing, and later obtain these products as needed at wholesale prices when you get orders and ship them or send if digital products. If you are selling products for affiliates, you can use affiliate links and direct orders to your affiliate for fulfillment and get a commission.

Another way to obtain products is through a product supplier like Aliexpress which you can add with an app like Oberlo. Aliexpress is one of the biggest wholesale suppliers of products for sale from online stores. It obtains its products from numerous manufacturers, much like Amazon features products from its vendors in its store.

Obtaining products from other suppliers might work if you have certain types of products, such as clothing, jewelry, toys, and stationery supplies. Then, you pick out items that compliment what you are already selling. If you have books on certain subjects, such as on health, beauty, or fashion, a related product line might be a good way to increase your sales.

I'll describe setting up product sales from an outside supplier in this chapter, using the Oberlo app to sell products from Aliexpress as an example.

Getting the Oberlo App

The Oberlo app is one of many apps available through the Shopify Apps store. To get it, go to the Shopify Apps link and click on it.

You may see some promotional ads when you first come to the app store.   You can ignore them unless you want to check them out. To get the Oberlo app, go to the Search bar and enter "Oberlo."

You will then get a description of the app. Click on "Get" to get it. You can start with a free trial offer for 30 days and after that pay $4.90 a month to continue.

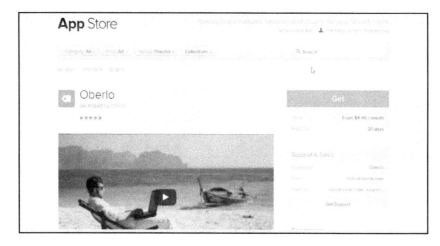

To make sure you really want to install the app, you'll get an advisory that you are about to install Oberlo, along with an explanation of what it does. If you still want to install it, click "Install App."

Next agree that after your free trial, to continue, you will pay $4.90 a month.

Then, you will get a "Welcome to Oberlo."

Pricing Your Products

After you join Oberlo, the next step is to set up your pricing rules, based on whether you want to use a multiplier based on your product's cost or prefer to mark up your product by a certain amount. Here's an example using a multiplier set to "2."

Alternatively, you can set up a specific product markup over your cost.

You can compare your proposed pricing with the manufacturer's suggested retail price.

You can use advancing pricing rules to consider different costs and markups to determine the best pricing for different products.

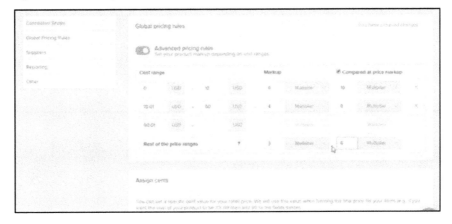

You can also set up your pricing to end in .95 or .99, which are popular price options.

When you are done, save your pricing settings.

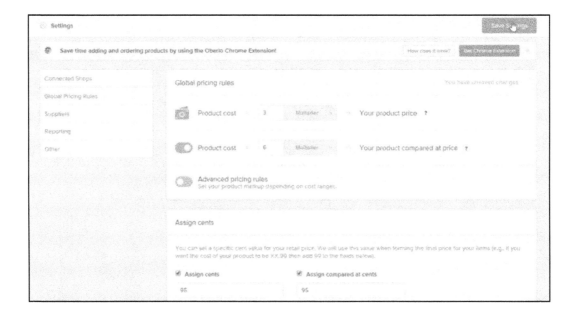

To make product importing and order fulfillment even easier, you can install an Oberlo Chrome extension. Then, with a single click, you can select a product and have it ready for customers to order from you.

If you opt to install this extension, you will get a request to add it. After you click that, you will get a notice that this extension has been added to Chrome.

Deciding on your pricing strategy can be a little complex, so experiment with different combinations. Even after you set up your store and begin selling, you can try different pricing levels of offers to find the price with the best returns and the most sales.

Selecting Products from Suppliers

Once you decide to add products from outside suppliers, Oberlo makes it very easy to do so. Just go back to the "Find and add your first product" link on your Oberlo dashboard and click the link to do that.

Then, click whatever category you want from the Aliexpress collection of products, where you will see all kinds of SuperDeals, Featured Brands, All Collections, Bestselling Products, New Tech Products, and Trending Styles.

You can select the type of products you want from the category list -- everything from clothing to electronics to jewelry, accessories, toys, health and beauty, and home improvement products. For example, if you choose jewelry, you'll see multiple types of jewelry products you can add to your store.

Once you click on a category, you'll see all kinds of products you can buy. In some cases, you can obtain the products with free shipping that you can pass on to your customer. In other cases, the shipping prices are listed, so you can incorporate that into your pricing.

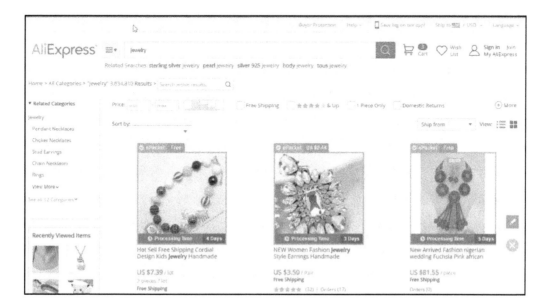

Aliexpress provides reviews of products and a seller's feedback score, so you can see how well the seller does in making a good product and shipping it in a timely fashion before you buy.

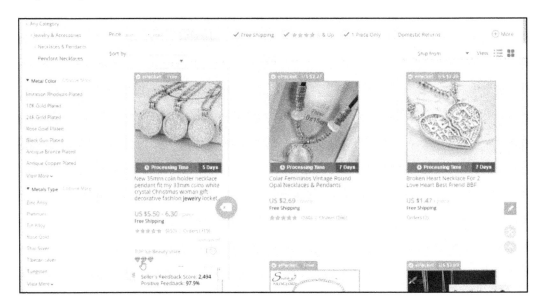

Once you are ready to buy, click on the item to see the terms and the number of orders that product has already received, along with shipping costs if any. Indicate the number of products you want to order, after which you will see the total price. To buy, click "Buy now." To add other items, click "Add to Cart" and buy them together.

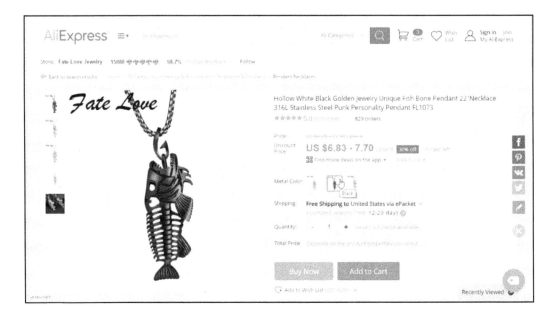

After you add something to your cart, you can continue shopping, view your cart, check all of the items in it, or buy everything now if you are ready. Once you have added everything you want to your cart, choose your shipping method.

To help you decide what to buy, you can sort the products within a category by the number of orders, the newest products listed, the seller rating, or the price from low to high or high to low.

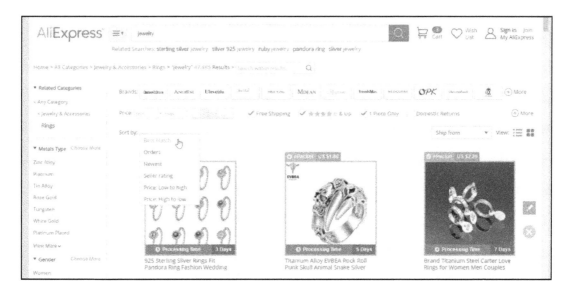

After your order is completed, when you go back to the Oberlo dashboard, you can go to your Import List to see the different products you ordered.

You'll see the different items in your queue.

If you scroll down, you'll see all of the items you added.

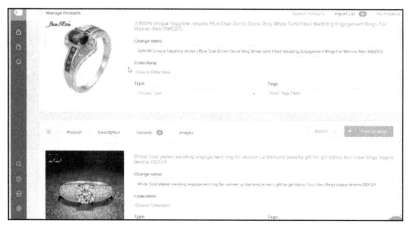

You can additionally customize the name of a product and add it to a collection.

If you click on the image, you will see a more detailed description of the product.

If you click on "variants," you will see the different varieties of the product which are available, such as in different colors, along with the number of products in inventory.

If you decide you don't want a particular product, you can remove it.

Once you are ready, you can push all of the products you have chosen into your shop. Then, you are done with your order.

You can also check your shop settings. If you have different shops for different product lines, they will be listed here.

You can set various store settings, such as being notified about new products.

You can be notified if a product or variant changes, or if there is a price or inventory change. Just click what you want to be notified about.

CHAPTER 6: CHOOSING A THEME

Either before or after you set up your products to sell, choose a theme to best display your products. I didn't select my theme until after my virtual assistant had added photos of all my books for sale. But I think it's a good idea to pick your theme first as well as decide on the collections in your store. This way you can set your products up in each collection, rather than having to rearrange them into collections later.

Here's an example of my initial page set up before I chose a theme.

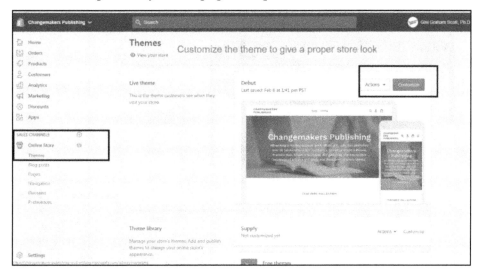

Once you think about themes, you can select from the Shopify theme store, where many themes are free while some have a charge – commonly $140 to $180. You can also select a theme from a third party store, and pay a fee for using that theme.

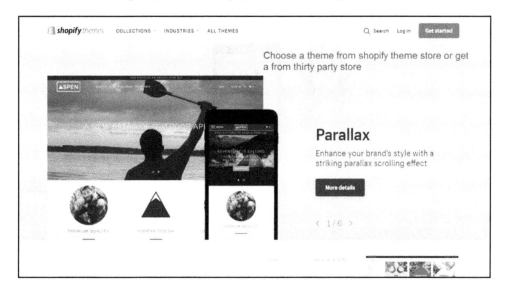

Selecting a Shopify Theme

A good way to look for themes is to start in the Shopify themes section -- either click through from your store or go to Shopify's theme page https://themes.shopify.com. The page starts off with six themes to consider, such as Boost and Pop.

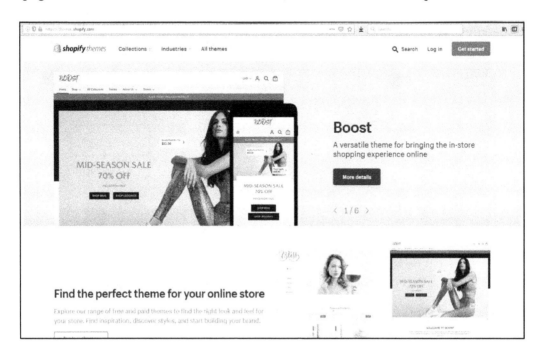

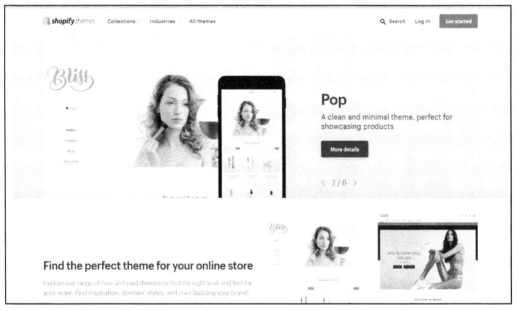

If you plan to sell clothing, there's Brooklyn:

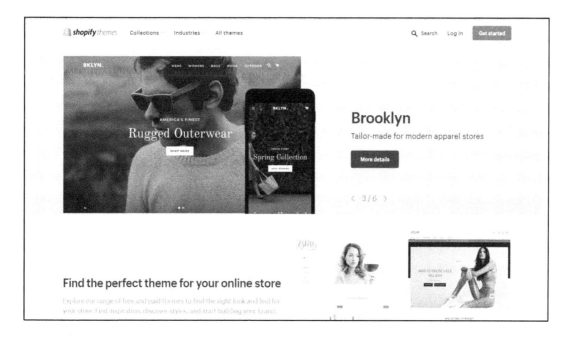

If you have lots of inventory, Shopify suggests their Capital theme.

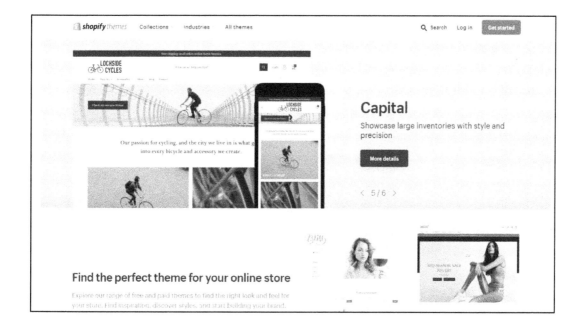

And Shopify invites you to explore its other available themes.

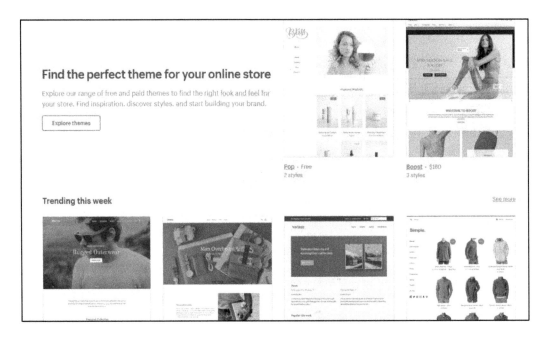

You can browse all of its themes -- currently 71 of them -- by price, the number of products, and layout style. Here the first themes listed are all paid themes -- $180 each, but you can select from free styles, too.

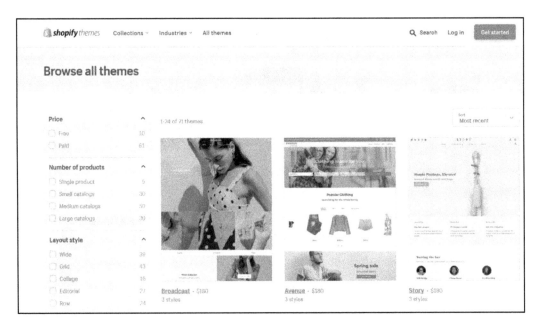

Here are the free themes sorted by popularity, though you can sort by the most recent. For the themes with a fee, you can sort from high to low or low to high.

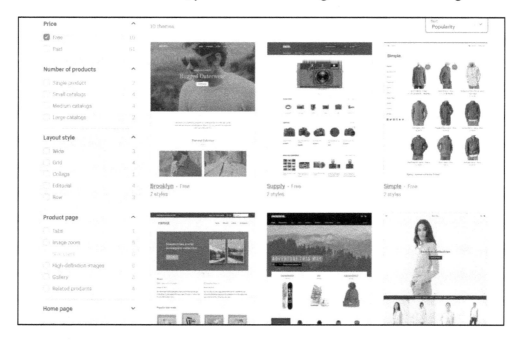

I liked the Minimal style, which I thought would be ideal for listing a series of book covers, so I chose that.

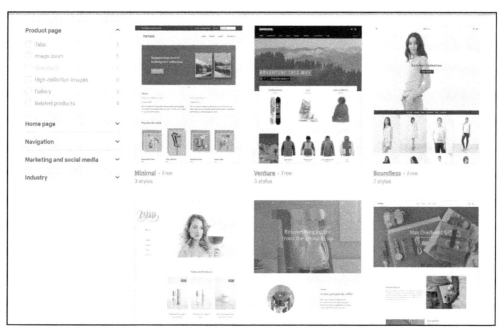

That style offered three variations: Vintage, Fashion, or Modern, and. I chose Modern.

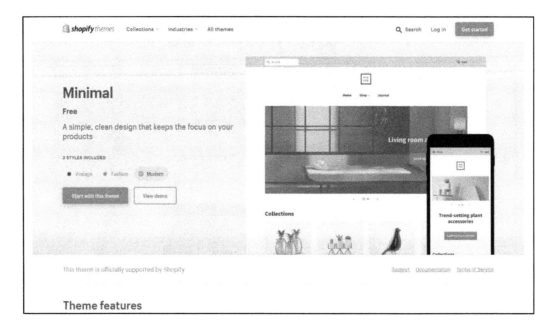

To help you choose your theme, Shopify includes a section on theme features. For instance, Modern permits a slide show, a product image zoom, a home page video, product filtering, and the ability to display related products from the same collection on your product pages.

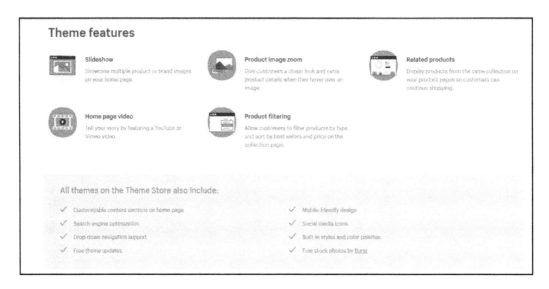

You can see examples of other stores using this theme.

Additionally, you can see customer ratings for the theme. If you already have a store set up, simply add that theme. If you have not yet started your store, you can choose this theme and start your 14 day free trial.

Most of the themes -- 61 out of 71 -- do have a fee, ranging from $140 to $180. Here are some examples of these themes at the low cost end at $140 each.

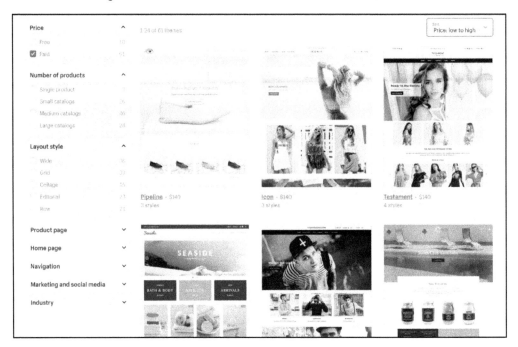

And here are some higher cost themes for $180 -- which seems especially suited for fashion.

The most popular themes are those that are free.

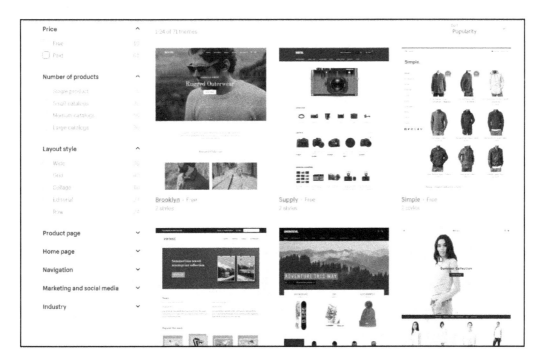

And here's what's most popular among the paid themes.

If you already set up your store, you will be invited to go to Shopify's online store to choose a theme. Go to "Launchpad Star" to start the process.

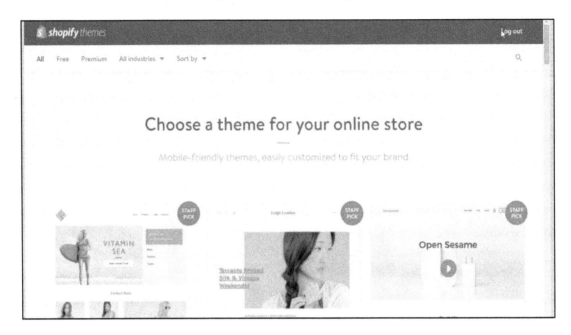

You will see the different choices as previously described, and will be invited to browse all of the free themes.

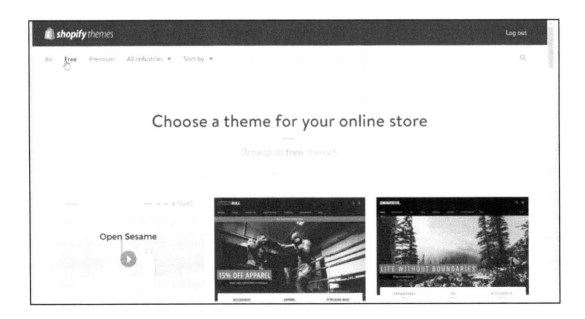

Whatever theme you choose, you will next install it.

Then, you'll see it downloading.

Customizing Your Theme

The next step is to go to the Theme Manager to customize your theme.

Then, customize your theme from your Theme Manager.

You'll see various options for making changes on your home page from the Pages section of your Shopify admin page. This includes editing the content on your home page and making changes in colors, typography, borders, headers, footer, product page, collection, categories, and more. The particular options available vary by the theme you choose.

For example, to customize the banner, you will see its length and width in pixels, so you can substitute a new banner of that size for the original.

You can choose among certain presets to select the overall color of the store.

You can also change the colors for the body text, accounts, links, and buttons, using a color palette to make the changes.

You can further customize the look of your store with typography:

You can additionally choose the style of font and size for the header, buttons, and body text. If you have a logo, you can upload that, too, as in the example below.

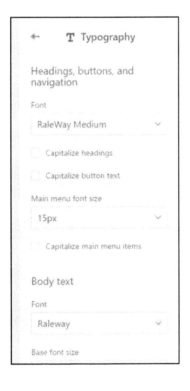

After that, you can incorporate your logo into your company header.

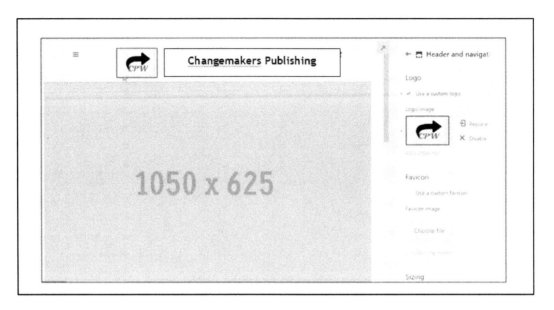

Then, for the footer, you can add custom content, invite visitors to sign up for a newsletter, and show any social media icons where you have accounts, such as Facebook, Twitter, and Instagram.

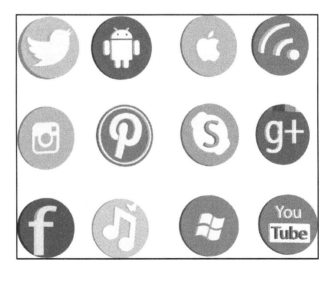

If you have a slide show, you can add it to your home page. You can show one slide after the other or use a fade effect, where one slide fades before the next appears.

Load your slide show with the first image. It will show up on your page.

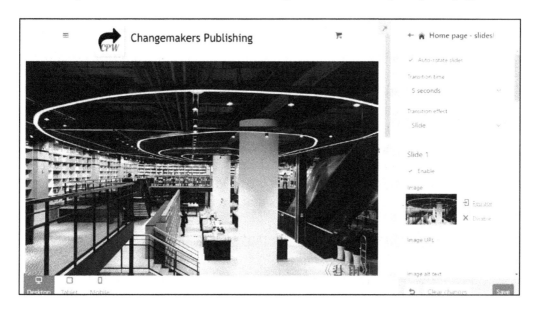

How to Pick the Best Theme for Your Store

When you choose and customize your theme, keep certain principles in mind to increase potential sales. You can do this before or after you upload products for your store, though it's a good idea to have your theme in place when you start organizing your products into collections. The theme you choose will help you decide what to place where.

In the previous section, I described a variety of themes offered by Shopify. You can also obtain third party themes from independent designers. But these can be more expensive and include more special bells and whistles, such as animating your store design. Such a unique look might be very dynamic, but it could slow down your store from loading quickly, which is a no-no for sales. If you are just starting out with your first store with a limited number of products, simple is better. The themes from Shopify incorporate these basic design principles of an effective store.

What theme works best? Here are some tips, inspired by an article on Shopify themes written by Andrew Roach: "Shopify Themes: How to Pick the Best Shopify Theme for Your Ecommerce Store."

1) **Your store theme should look familiar, so it has a simple, conventional design with commonly used layouts.** This way you clearly indicate what you are selling, and have the kind of product photo, description, price, and other information about the product clearly presented. By following common design principles, you help make buyers comfortable buying from you.

2) **Some of the good design features include the following:**
   a. A product image that highlights the product, and if appropriate, an image that shows the product in use. If it's a product like a book or CD, just a cover image is fine; but many other products benefit from showing an active user, such as a skier using ski equipment.
   b. A clear call-to-action on the page, such as a "buy now" button.
   c. An interactive product page, where the prospective customer can move a cursor around the image and click to zoom in to look at the product more closely. Another option might be for the customer to browse through different pictures of a product or related products with a few clicks.
   d. A detailed description of what the product offers, next to the product.
   e. A way to get to other products that are part of the same product line or are similar products.
   f. An opportunity to click on the plus sign next to "details" to learn even more about the product
   g. A way to add your email address on the same page, so the prospective customer can sign up for more updates on products from you.

3) **Take your budget into consideration in choosing a theme**. Start simply and inexpensively if you are just getting started or have a limited budget. The free Shopify themes take into consideration the basic design principles and are fine.

4) **A good approach is a simple layout with a banner, which you might create from a stock photo or collage of product shots**. For instance, I plan to create a layout in Photoshop with a half-dozen of my books on different subjects using Shopify's "Minimal" design with the Modern style. If you don't have the budget, time, or designer skills to create an attractive banner, you can choose a Shopify theme which focuses on the products.

5) **Use high quality product images if you have them**. If not, avoid using a template which features large product images. A series of smaller images will work better.

6) **Select a theme which is mobile friendly**, since Shopify has found that over 50% of sales from its stores occur on mobile devices. Additionally, check out the mobile experience of users after you set up some products on your site. This way, if your theme doesn't work well for your prospective customers, you can choose another. In doing this mobile check, look at your store's appearance on both a smartphone and a tablet.

7) **Avoid complicated Shopify website templates which have unnecessary features,** like fancy scrollers and animations, which slow down the website. Though some visitors may find such features appealing, the page will take longer to load, which will be a turn-off for many would-be buyers.

8) **Though you are generally safest choosing a theme available through Shopify, you can find more unique themes through third party designers and from WordPress**, which enables you to build a Shopify website.

9) **Two of the easy to use themes for a beginner which Shopify recommends** are Jumpstart, which is ideal for one or two products, and Brooklyn, which is idea for a general webstore. Also, check out Minimal, which is what I chose to start with.

10) **Get your own website.com domain**, since it will make your store appear more professional and increase your conversion rate.

11) **The most important elements to include on your page include the following**:
- Product images
- Price tags
- A clear Call-to-Action (CTA) button, usually one that says "Add to Cart", which means you have set up a purchase arrangement on the backend, such as with PayPal
- A display of all relevant information without cluttering the page
- A product description, along with any specifics, such as different versions, sizes, or types
- Delivery information
- Return/refund information

Ideally, use separate tabs below the product to display this information, but you can use a simple description tab with these details, too.

12) **Use your product page to lead to other pages in your store**. You can use a related products section if your Shopify theme has that. If not, you can add a free Shopify App that leads to other pages.

13) **To increase trust in your store and provide more value toprospective customers, add social proof in the form of reviews**. You can also obtain a security badge through Shopify: This badge shows that your store meets Payment Card Industry (PCI) standards.

14) Provide a good category page which provides a clear title and navigation sidebar listing the various categories or collections in your product line. Here are some examples of pages which feature these categories or collections.

15) **Have a good homepage**. This is very important because this is the most commonly visited page by new customers, repeat customers, and referrals. The page should include the following:

- Feature your latest products, which is especially important for engaging returning visitors.
- Provide a showcase for your best sellers.
- Clearly show how your store will provide benefit and value to buyers.
- Include elements that inspire trust, such as security badges and positive reviews.
- Have an attractive banner. This banner could be a slider with a series of changing images, if you have the time and resources to make a great looking slider or can hlre someone make it for you. Alternatively, feature a single strong image on your banner, such as someone using your product or an image showing your product or brand identity. For example, if you are selling books or products related to spirituality, a priest or worshipper meditating in a forest with a glowing light might convey the essence of your line of products. Rather than have a few changing images for your banner, some say a single banner works the best in converting interest into sales.

CHAPTER 7: ORGANIZING YOUR PRODUCTS INTO COLLECTIONS

A major key to success is organizing your products into collections based on categories or types of products, so prospective customers can more easily find what they are looking for. The process is much like you will see in any store, such as when there are sections of jackets, sports coats, business suits, casual pants, dress pants, and so on. Additionally, if you have a large inventory, you can further divide collections into subcategories, such as by price for a luxury line, a moderately priced line, and low cost bargain line. Decide on the categories or collections that are most suited to your type of business.

The Basics of Adding Products to a Collection

To organize your products into collections, consider the products you already have and the types of products you want to add in the near future. You can always add additional categories as your inventory expands.

You can go to "Products" and then "All Products" to see your complete listing. If you have a number of products in stock, the "Inventory" listing will show the name of items in stock and list the number of variants, such as for different styles or sizes, if applicable. I'm selling print-on-demand books, so "Inventory" doesn't apply. "Type" of product refers to the overall category, such as "books" or "jewelry". Finally, the listing includes the vendor for that product, which in this case is me.

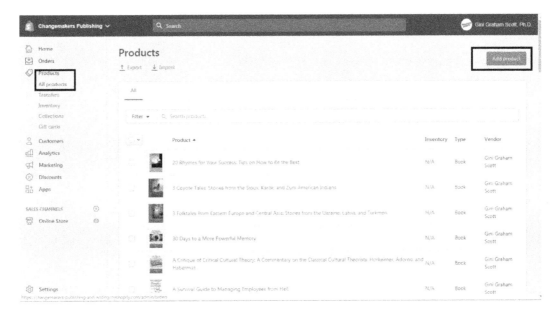

To add your products to collections, first enter each product's title and description, as previously discussed.

Then, as previously noted, indicate the product price and information about the number of products in inventory, if you are directly carrying the stock or can readily obtain it in a day or two. Otherwise, leave this blank.

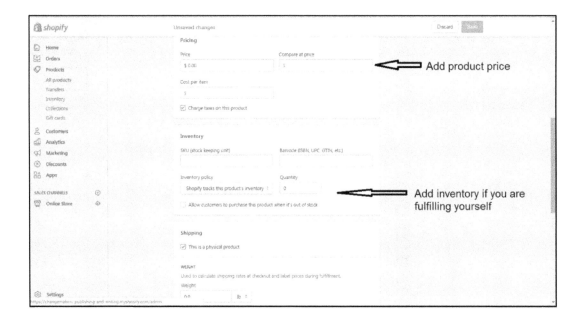

After listing and describing your products, indicate the product's title and conditions. Later, you can use those conditions to help you designate what product belongs in what collection.

Also give each collection a name. For instance, my collections will be based on the type of book (i.e.: sales and marketing, self-help, social trends). You can use simple descriptive names (i.e.: necklaces, rings) or more detailed descriptions, if you have a number of products in a category (i.e.: pearl necklaces, diamond necklaces, novelty necklaces). For certain types of products, use a catchy name (i.e.: Classic Combos, Look the Part Jeans, Get that Promotion Business Suits).

You can also add products to a collection automatically by creating a tag for your collection. Then, all products with that tag will be added to that collection.

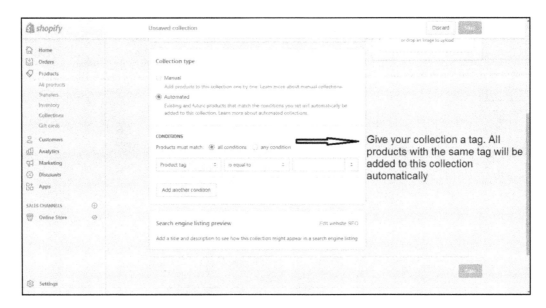

A Step-by-Step Guide to Creating Your Collections

Now that you know the basics of creating your collections, here's a step-by-step guide about what to do. To start a collection, go to the Products/Collections section.

After you click "add collection," give the collection a title and description.

After that, set the conditions for adding products to your collection. You can add them manually, which means you decide what products to add yourself. Or you can easily add them automatically, based on the way you tag your products and the conditions you have set for the products in a collection.

For example, you can automatically set up a product to be added to a collection if it meets any or all conditions. Then, you specify the particular conditions, such as having a certain product title, type, vendor, price, tag, weight and so on.

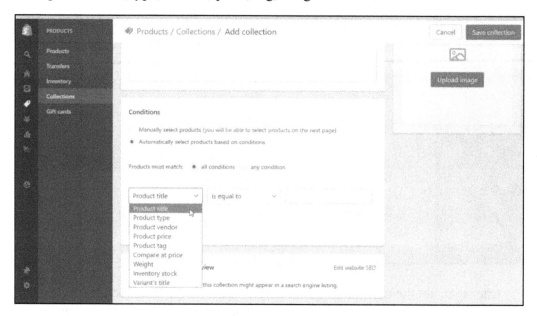

You also indicate whether the listed product characteristic, such as the title or type, contains or is equal to a particular category. The example below shows where a product title must contain the word "necklace" to be included in the necklace collection.

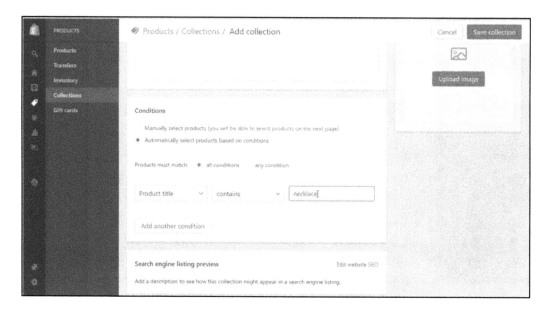

Then, you will see the selected product in the listing of products in that collection. You'll see a thumbnail image for each product, plus a description, such as in the example below that shows some product listings for self-help books.

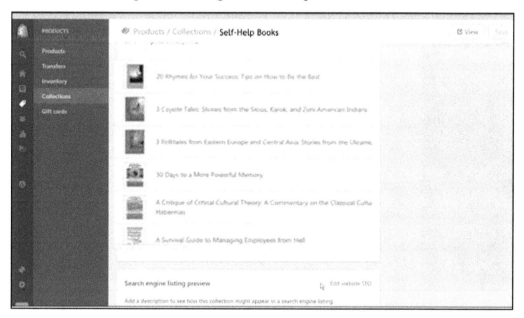

Once you create your collection, you'll get a notice that it was created successfully, and you'll be asked to set its description and conditions, plus add an image to represent the collection. You can also view your collection in your store or create another collection. For instance, if I was creating a collection of necklaces rather than books, this is the message I would get.

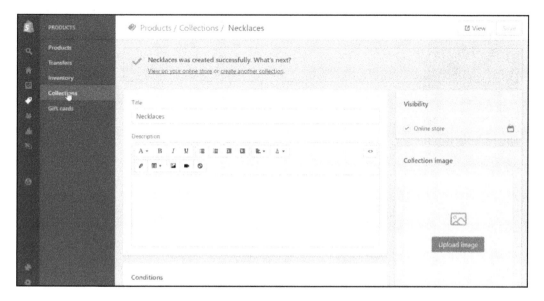

You can add as many collections as you want. Go to the Collections tab under products and click on Add Collection. Then, go to the Add Collection page, where you will get the menu to describe the collection you want to add.

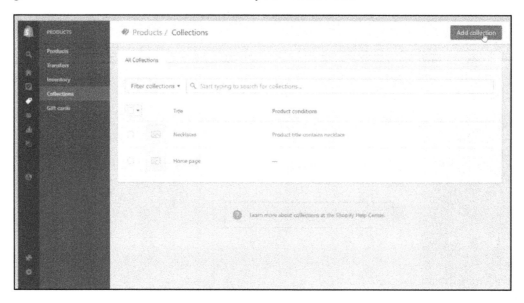

As before, you can indicate the condition, such as a word or name the title will contain and any word or name it won't. For instance, if I'm creating a collection of books on "success" in business, I want to include that word, and since this nonfiction, I might indicate that I don't want to include a "novel". Each time you create a collection, add an image for that collection, which could be one of your products, or use another image or logo to characterize that collection as a whole.

You can also set up a collection of "Featured" products, where you can include products in other collections. Specify the conditions to be featured and upload an image for the collection.

If you prefer to select products manually rather than specifying the conditions to add a product to a collection you can do that, too. Just indicate that you want to select your products manually. Then, you can search for products to add on the next page in your store.

Now, you can find the products you want to add.

To deal with a group of selected products at the same time, you can choose assort bulk actions, such as publishing, hiding, or deleting the selected products. You can also add or remove tags, and add or remove selected products from the collection.

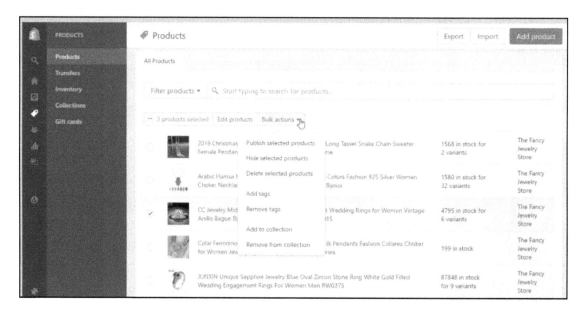

Once you choose to add a product to a collection, you will be asked which collection, such as your featured collection.

To reorder more of a product, go the collection where it is. You can find it manually by name or by going to your products which are listed by bestselling, by the first letter from A-Z or Z-A, by price from highest to lowest or lowest to highest, or by date from newest to oldest or oldest to newest.

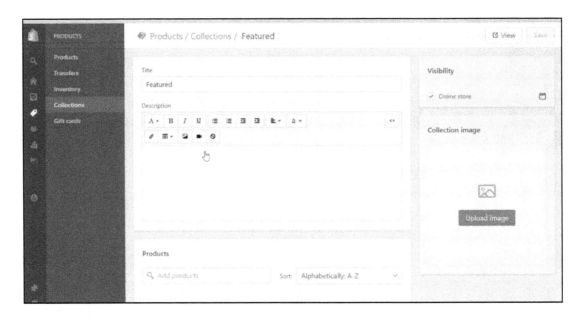

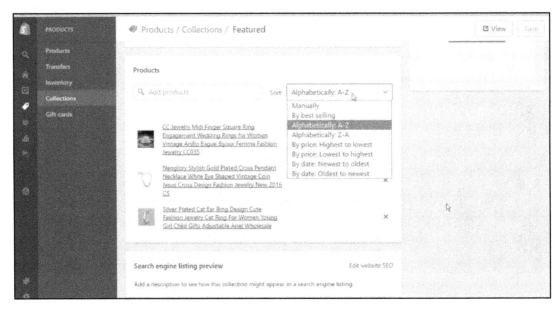

You can organize the items to be added manually, too. In doing so, you can change the order of products by clicking on a product bar on the left and dragging a product to a different position. This is shown in a comparison of these screen shots, where the top images have moved to the bottom of three images. In the third image, the top two images have switched places. Should you want to remove an item, click the "X."

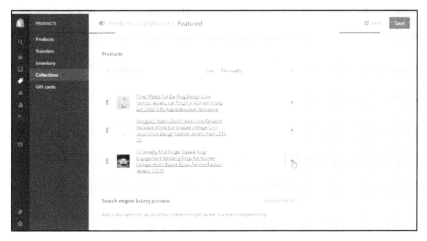

You can select products based on pricing, whether the price is greater or less than a certain amount. To include everything, set the greater than price to "$0.00."

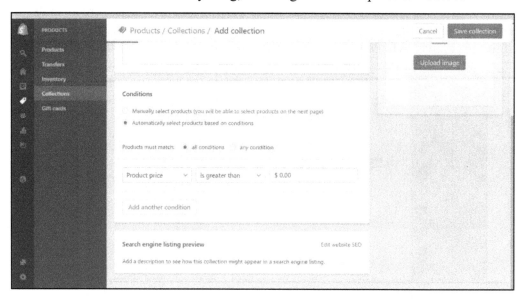

To feature your latest products, organize your collection from newest to oldest. You can also create a separate category for your "New" products, just like you can create one for "Featured" products. In some cases, there may be some overlap, where you feature a new product, but that's fine. This double listing can increase your sales when your potential customer sees your product again. If you go to Netflix, you'll see this approach used when the same new release is include in "Newly Released," "Trending," and categories by topic, such as "Crime Thrillers."

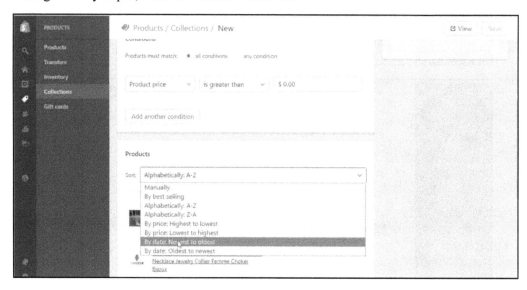

CHAPTER 8: GETTING PAYMENTS

Once you have your store set up and are ready to take orders, the next step is setting up a method to receive payments and handle shipping and order fulfilment. You can read more about Shopify's payment policies if you go to Settings.

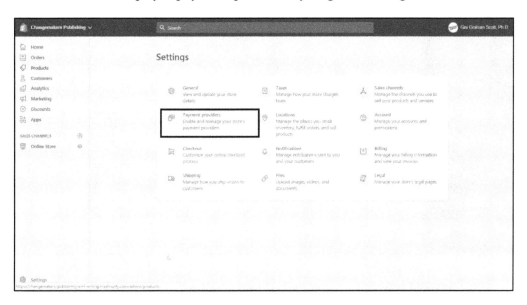

To receive payments, set up your payment options indicating whether you accept credit cards, PayPal, Amazon Pay, Shopify Payments, or other payment methods.

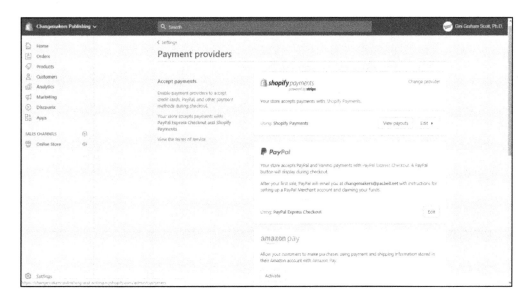

If you accept PayPal payments, you will see various options for using PayPal, as well as using credit cards through PayPal. You first need a PayPal business account which is easy to set up through PayPal with a linked and verified checking account. Then, you have to give Shopify third-party API access to your PayPal profile.

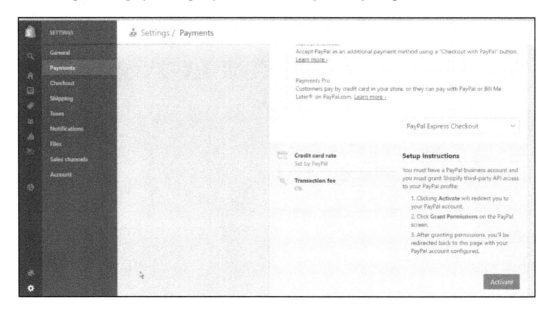

You'll see the following screen advising you to log in with PayPal to set up permissions for your account.

You'll next see a series of prompts to grant permission to Shopify. These include using Express Checkout to process payments and enabling Shopify to process credit or debit card payments and provide refunds to customers who want to return a purchase. Additionally, Shopify wants permissions to capture your PayPal transactions, charge a customer based on prior transactions, accept or deny a pending transaction, and access your PayPal contact information. Normally, you will provide permission for everything, though you can select certain permissions now. Later, you can always change or revoke any permission you have granted. Once you check the permissions you want to grant, click Grant Permissions.

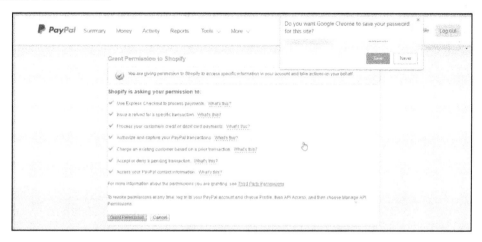

Should you want to accept credit cards through Shopify, which means Shopify can transfer money from your sales to your bank account, complete the account set up for that. Go to the Settings/Payments page and complete the Shopify Complete Account Setup section.

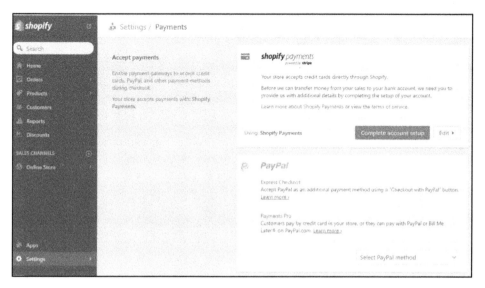

Next, fill in information about your business, your business address, and state.

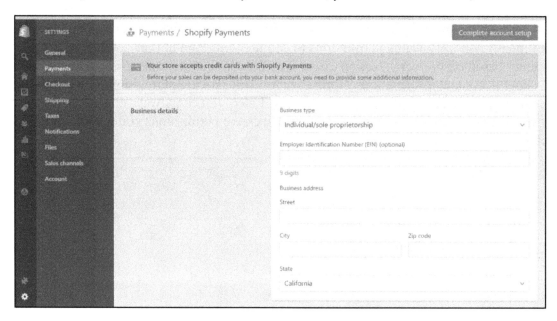

Then, add some personal details, including your date of birth and Social Security number in order to verify your identity. After that, add product details about your sales and products being sold. These include your average order price and average shipping time.

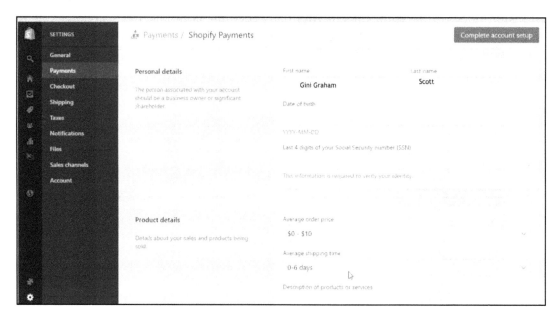

Finally, indicate the billing statement for each customer, along with your banking account information.

Now you are set up to get orders. Just fill in the customer billing for each payment you expect to receive for an order. After you have received payment, you need to be ready to ship that product or arrange for another party to ship it for you.

CHAPTER 9: SHIPPING

To set up your shipping, go to "Shipping" in your settings.

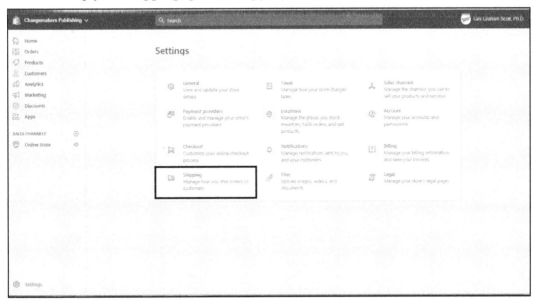

Set up your shipping origins and your rates for domestic shipping and the rest of the world. Start by selecting a shipping zone.

You will then see various options for shipping, such as if you want to use UPS.

You will also see different options for rates, such as if you want to use price or weight based shipping or calculated rates.

Here's an example of how you might set this up, where I have indicated the shipping origins from Changemakers Publishing. I have added in different shipping charges for standard shipping and for heavy packages. These charges get added on to the cost of goods shipping. For instance, I have charged $5, which is the average cost of sending a single book, and $10 for larger shipments, since each additional book is about $2 more.

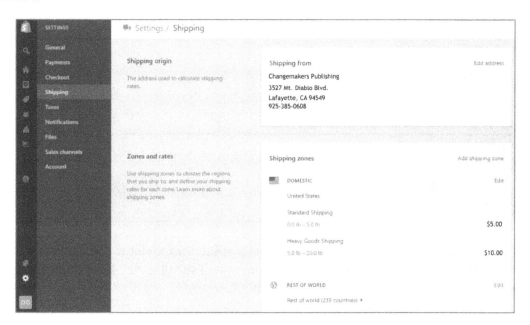

You can edit those prices at any time should shipping rates change.

As an alternative, you can use a price based rate for shipping, as indicated below.

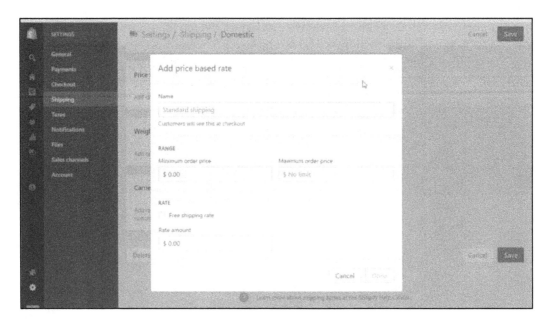

If you have a special offer, such as free shipping for regular orders delivered with a certain time frame, indicate this. Then, customers will see that they have qualified for this offer and have not been charged for shipping.

If a customer wants a faster delivery, set a shipping price for Express Shipping, as in the example below.

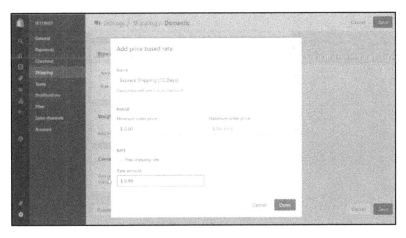

After you set these prices, you will see all of the options you have set up.

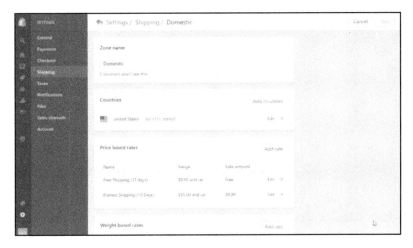

After setting up domestic shipping, you can set up the cost of shipping to the rest of the world, which now includes about 240 countries (the number varies depending on when you ship.

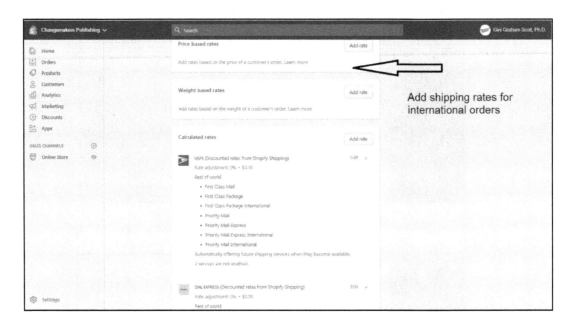

Click edit to set up price based, weight based, or carrier-calculated rates.   After you enter each type of pricing, you will see the different options (i.e.: free or express shipping) below.

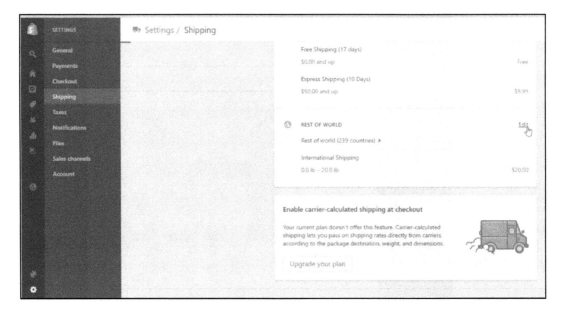

And here are more options.

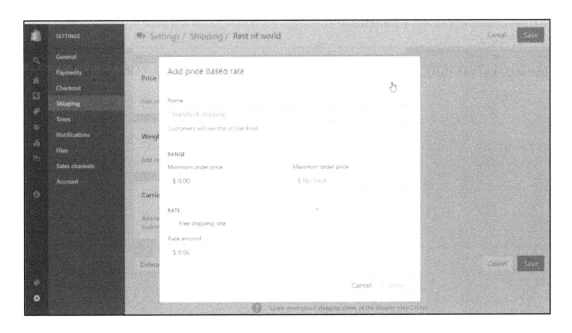

As with domestic shipping, you can set up both standard and express shipping rates. Take into consideration the way prices vary for different countries, and set a single price that will apply to all countries,

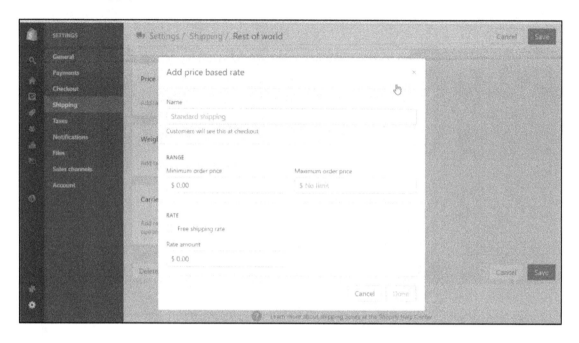

Once you have everything set up, you will see a summary of the shipping rates you have established for both domestic shipping and for the rest of the world.

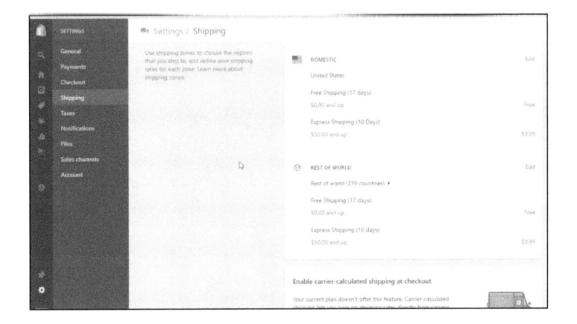

CHAPTER 10: ORDER FULFILLMENT

Once you have set up your payment and shipping arrangements, you can begin fulfilling orders — whether you do it yourself or arrange for someone else to do it. If another party does it for you, figure on either paying an hourly payment rate if someone works for you or set a per item or per order price for independent subcontractors. If you get a large number of orders, you can ideally outsource this since the costs in other countries are much less, such as in India, Pakistan, Indonesia, and the Philippines. You can often find such workers through Fiverr, Upwork, or other freelance services.

To set up an order, go to "Orders." Indicate the order number, customer, the payment, how you are fulfilling the order, and the price.

Click on the title you have given for that order to see details about it, including any tax.

You also need to create the shipping label, which you can set up to print automatically for each order.

Additionally, add in information about the box size and weight. If you are shipping multiple items, you will see a summary. If there is only one item, as in this test order, there is nothing to summarize.

As an alternative to printing your own labels, you can buy packing labels. After you do so, the order will be fulfilled with your shipping charges included in your order.

CHAPTER 11: ADDING APPROPRIATE APPS

After you set up your store, you can obtain the appropriate apps from the Shopify App Store. These can help you grow your business by suggesting products you can add; print orders, labels, and receipts; run efficiently run better Facebook ads; share your customer reviews; and more.

You can find the apps that are best suited to your business if you do a search by your type of products. You can search by name or category. Before you start your search, you'll see staff picks and products recommended for you. For example, PriceSpy shows you what competitors are charging for similar products so you can match them. CrossSellPro offers also bought recommendations. Product Waiting Lists recommends related products you might sell, and Advanced Shipping Rules offers guidelines on shipping your products more effectively.

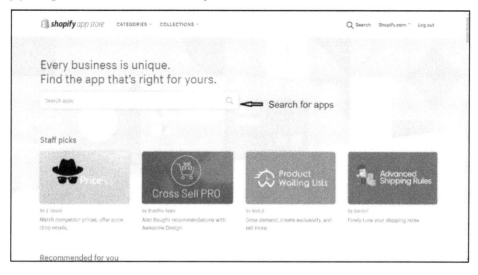

To learn more about an app, click on it. If you want to add it to your store, click "Add app."

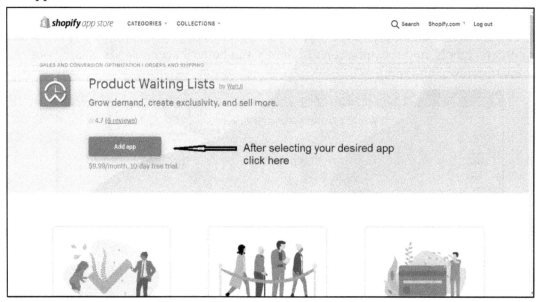

The final step is to install the app. You will get additional information about what the app will do, such as viewing your account details, managing your products and customers, and better managing your online store. If you decide to install the app, click "Install app," and that's it.

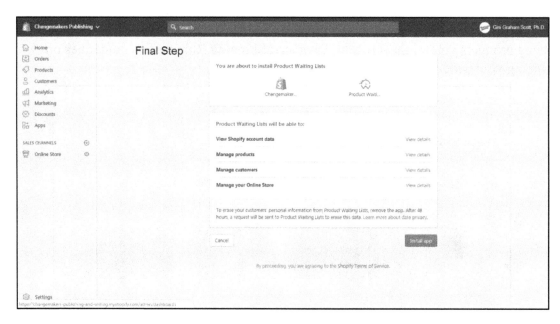

Shopify will also recommend some featured apps when you go to the App Store, as well as point out "New and Noteworthy" apps. Here are examples of other apps you might consider installing.

One of its featured apps, Kopigin, will help you generate unique product descriptions for your store.

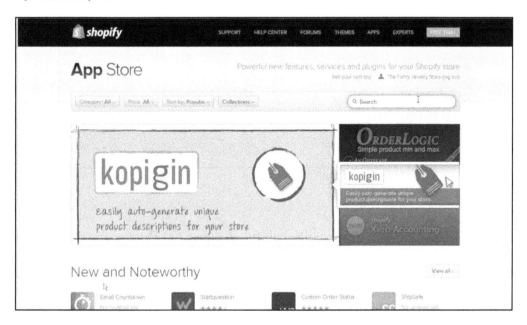

SEO Doctor will help increase your SEO ranking.

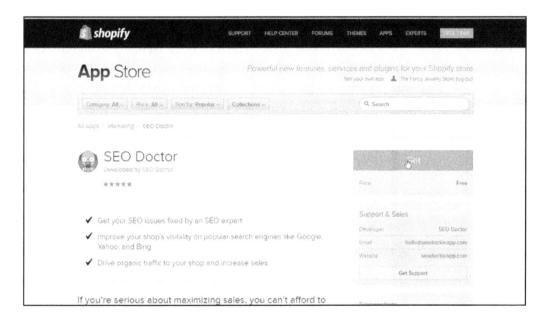

As before, you get the app and then install it.

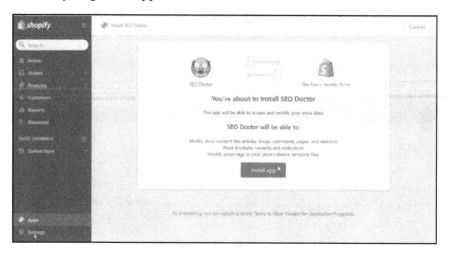

SEO Doctor

The SEO Doctor app is especially helpful. As the SEO Doctor app description indicates, the app will help you analyze the different components of your store, so you can know what is working well and what to improve for a better SEO ranking. This better ranking will help prospective customers find your store easily. SEO Doctor additionally enables you to automatically diagnose and fix your store's SEO issues with its Autopilot Feature. This will help you improve your shop's ranking on popular search engines like Google, Bing, and Yahoo. Also, this Smart Automation feature will drive organic traffic to your shop and reduce the amount of time you spend on SEO.

More specifically, here are some things you can do with SEO Doctor and why its is a good app to get for your store. It can review each of your webpages, and analyze how well that page is performing for you. You can do an audit of different categories.

You can check on the performance of individual products.

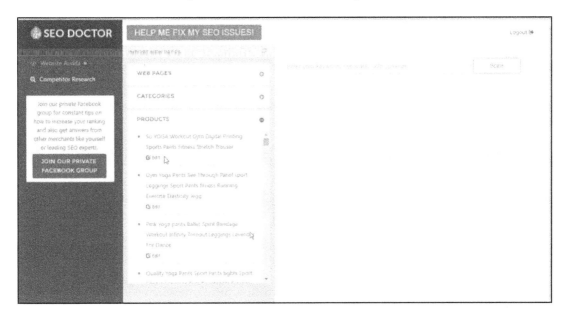

You can do an audit of your home page.

To do the audit, put in a keyword for the page, scan, and see the results. You'll learn how quickly the page loads, which should be less than 5 seconds, and you shouldn't have more than 15 grammatical mistakes.

If you discover such problems, you can fix them, such as reducing the number of photos or uploading lower resolution photos for a faster load time. You'll also learn if the URL for your site is SEO friendly, which occurs if the exact keyword is found in that URL. As SEO Doctor prescribes, it's best to include targeted keywords in the URL for your store, since it makes you more findable, because this keyword helps potential visitors identify the topic of your page from your URL.

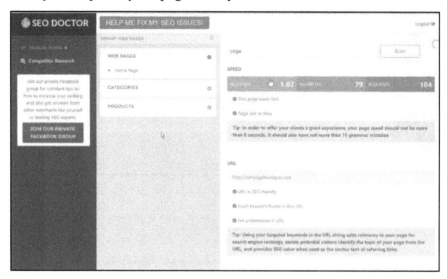

SEO Doctor additionally provides your SEO score, based on a variety of factors, such as loading space, use of keywords, visitors to your page, and more. A perfect score is 100%; a 74.5% as in the example below is pretty good.

Another advantage of this program is it will give you tips on what to do to make your store even better, such as having a good title tag which includes a keyword for your type of product line. Such a tag makes a big difference for your findability, since search engines consider your title tag to be the most important place for your keyword to appear.

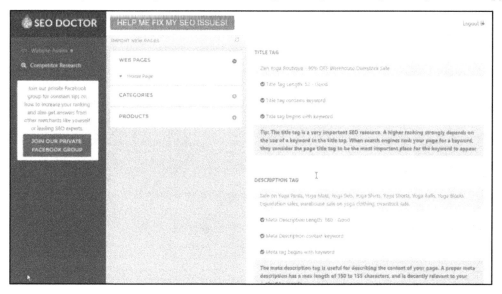

Additionally, the program will do an image analysis, and it recommends using "alt attributes" which identify an image with keywords that increase the page rankings. In case this image identification is unfamiliar to you, an "alt attribute" specifies an alternate text or information for an image, if the image cannot be displayed, such as when a user cannot view it due to a slow connection or using a screen reader.

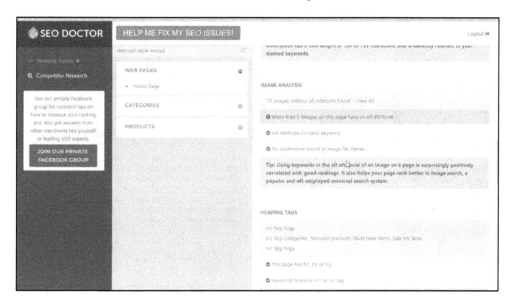

SEO Doctor can also analyze the effectiveness of your heading tags, including noting if you have duplicate tags you should remove. Other recommendations include using keywords in each of your headers one or two times but not more, and keeping your content to over 300 characters (about 30 words) and using keywords every 100 words.

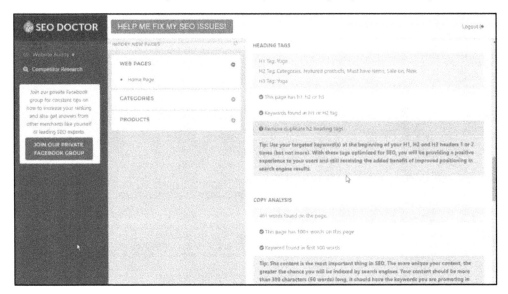

SEO Doctor additionally will conduct a social media analysis and let you know where you are lacking so you can improve. This analysis will include your presence on Twitter and Facebook, and it will suggest what you can do to better promote your store, such as by adding a Google Plus button and interacting with your social following to get them engaged with you.

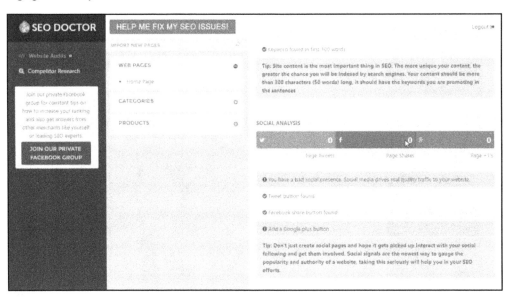

Another analysis considers whether your site is mobile friendly, meaning that it is responsive and adjusts well to being viewed on a mobile phone or laptop, since about a half or more customers now use mobile devices to buy.

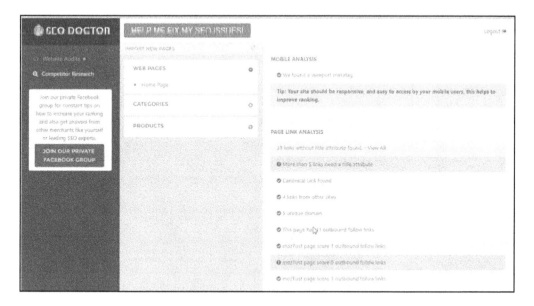

SEO Doctor conducts a root domain analysis, too, which involves assessing how many backlinks you have to your site -- in other words, how many other sites are linking to you, with the more the merrier! Think about who you know with whom you can trade links with, or invite people to link to your page and become followers. On the other hand, you don't want to have too many links following other websites. Don't have more than 100, since then it appears that you are indiscriminately linking to other sites.

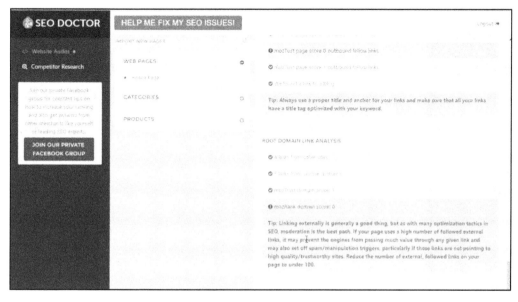

Another analysis is of your own domain. In this analysis, SEO Doctor makes recommendations on how to increase your SEO, including getting a Google site and Bing verification. This helps Google's search engine better understand and rank your website. Should some of these analyses become too technical, you can consult with an SEO expert to help improve your site.

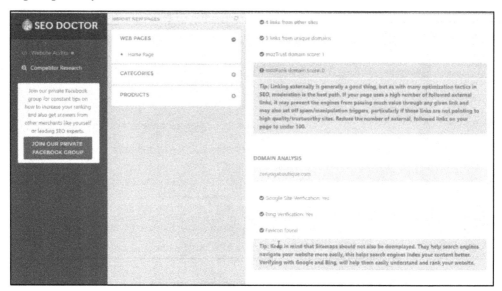

You can additionally use SEO Doctor to do a competitive analysis of your store and others, based on your location, type of products, and other factors. To start the process, put in your URL, a competitor URL, and a keyword. Then, look at how you compare how you are doing based on that keyword. For example, I might compare my bookstore to another Shopify bookstore.

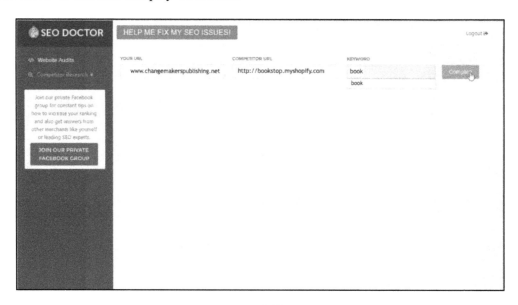

In doing this comparison, SEO Doctor will give you feedback on how your score ranks and do a side by side comparison with the competing site.

In short, SEO Doctor is a very helpful app to assess how well your store is doing and what you can do to improve it.

FinditQuick Shopping Network

Another helpful app if you are looking for popular products to add to your store is the FindItQuick Shopping network. Go to the App Store and search for "FindItQuick."

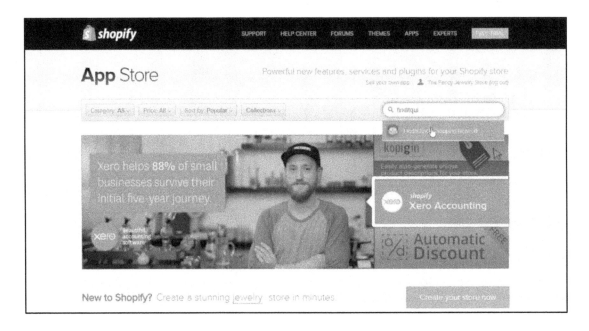

Next, get it and install it.

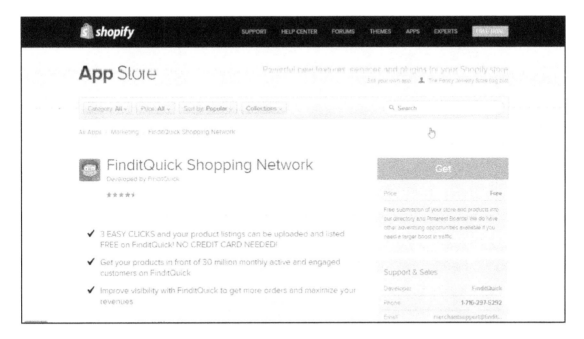

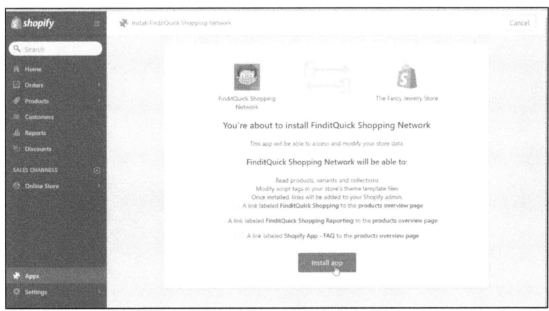

Once it's installed, you can look for products.

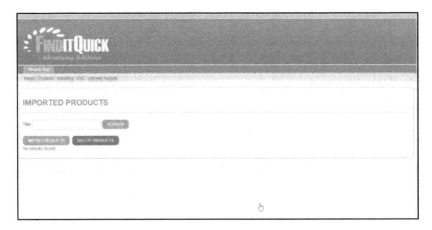

Import what you want for your store. You can select a series of products to import, and FindItQuick will let you know when they are all there.

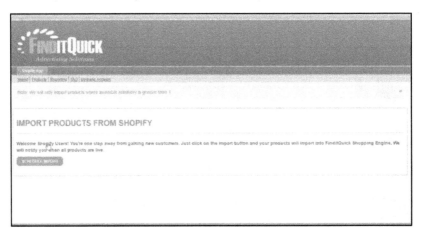

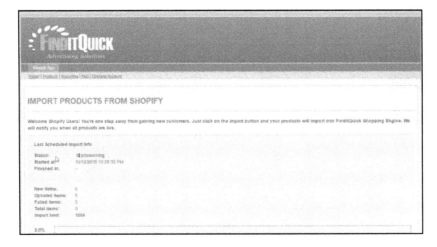

Once your order is complete, FindItQuick let you know and indicate the number of new items you have imported.

Then, you can see all the products you added to your store. If a product is doing well, you can bump it up to the top of your email promotions for your store. Additionally, you can see an activity report showing how well different products are doing.

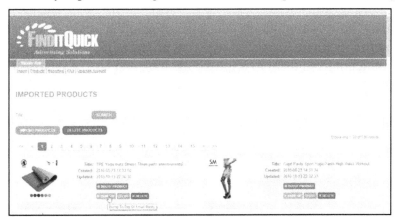

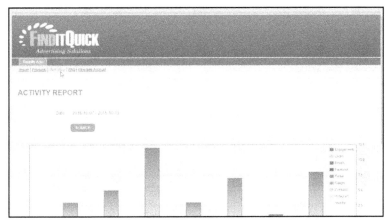

If you do a search for the keyword for your shop, you can see how well it is doing in that category.

To compare how your products and store compare to others in your niche, go to the top selling stores in your category to see what products they are advertising and how. This way you can learn from them to improve the look and feel of your store and the product you carry.

Varinode Ads

Another useful app is Verinode Ads, which enables you share traffic with other stores and reach new customers interested in your products. The site gives you analytics, so you can see how your ads are performing, and it helps you create new ads that might perform better for you. Another benefit is that it's a free ad exchange so it's an inexpensive way to grow your business.

To get started, go to the Shopify App Store, look for Varinode Ads, and install the app.

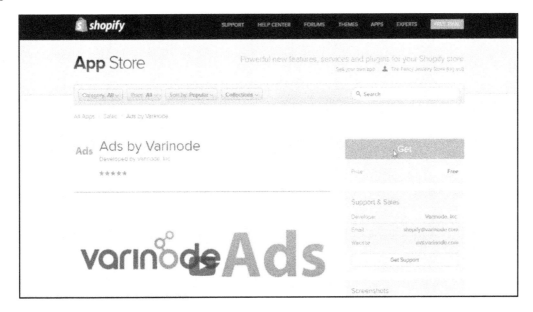

To start the ad swapping process, answer some questions about your store. Indicate the category and subcategory which are the best fit for you. Additionally, indicate the gender of your primary market, if this is the case.

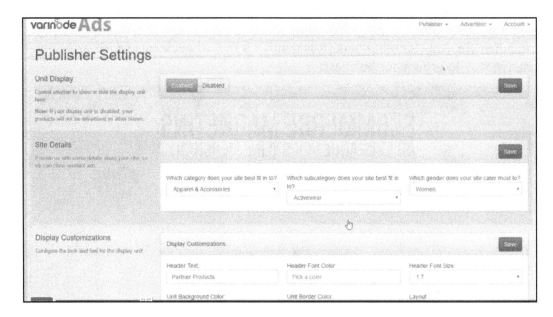

Shopify has a list of categories and subcategories you can choose from.

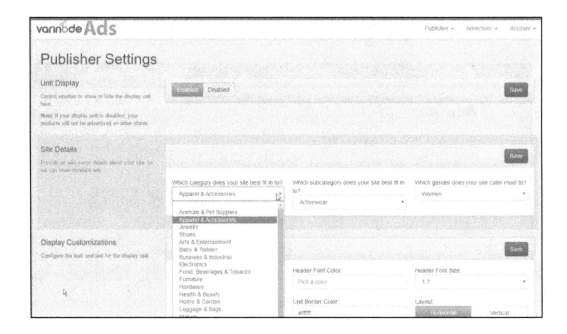

Customize the details indicating how you would like your ad to be displayed. This example shows your ad in the category of jewelry and the subcategory of jewelry appealing primary to women. You can also indicate the text of the header, the font color, the number of items to display, and more.

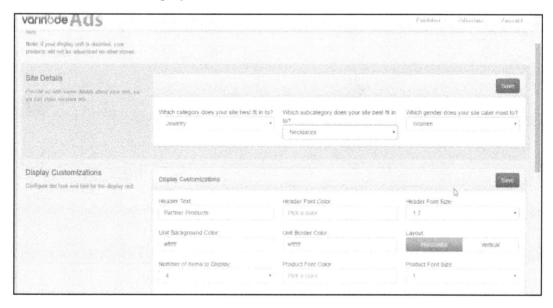

Then, you'll see how your ad will appear along with ads for your partners.

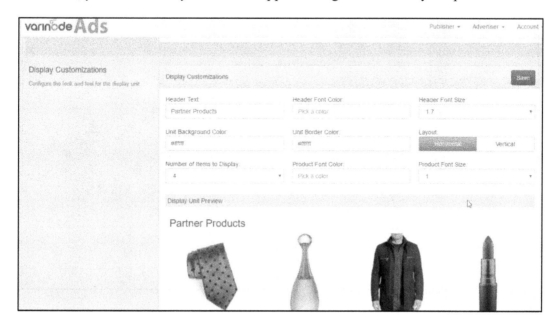

If you like the way your ad appears, save your settings.

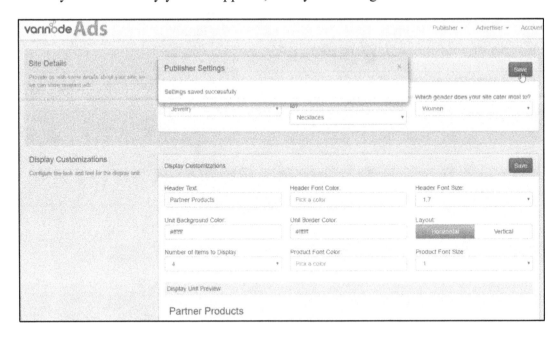

After your campaign has been running for a while, you can see how your ads are doing.

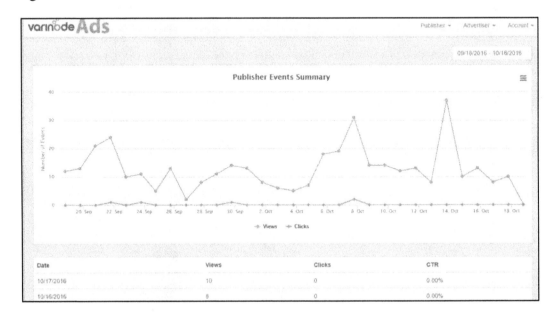

You'll also see your available ad credits to use in making an ad exchange.

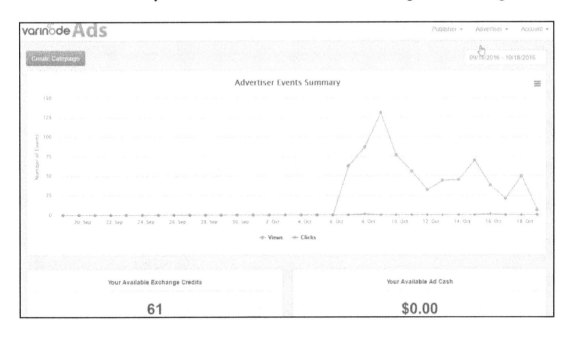

In an ad exchange, you use your credits that you want to bid. Include your campaign name, the number of credits you are bidding, your daily budget, and your start and end dates.

Varinode Ads also provides a campaign summary of your current campaign, indicating the number of views and clicks you have received. The summary indicates this is an exchange ad, the maximum credits you have bid, and your schedule if your campaign is continuing. To create another ad, click the Create Your Ad button.

Here's a brief overview of how creating an ad for the exchange process works. You look for products in your category, ideally at least five, as Shopify recommends. An additional requirement is that you can't set up your store behind a password.

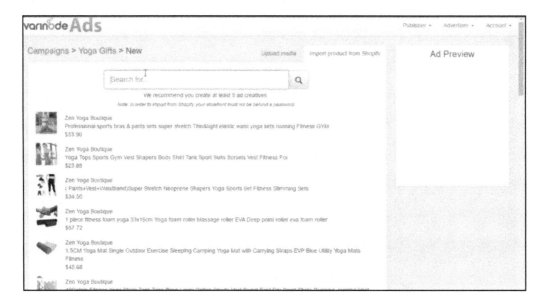

Once you get a list of recommended products, select a product from the list, such as the yoga mat below.

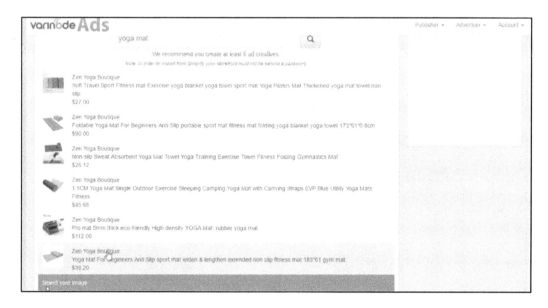

If the product is available in multiple colors, choose one image for the ad.

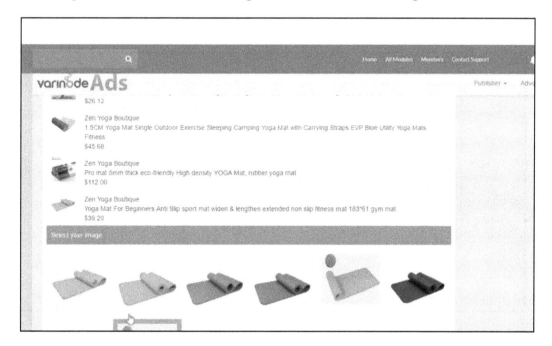

Next indicate the product's title and description. Include the URL where it appears and the price. Target the ad by category, subcategory, and the gender of the primary customer. To target a particular country for your campaign, indicate that, too.

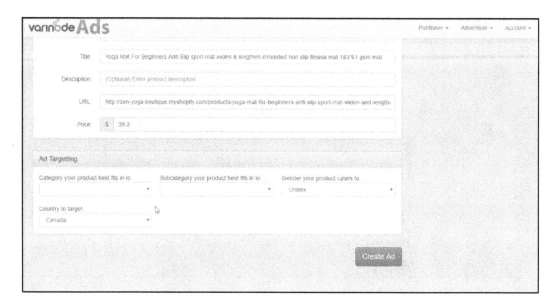

Then, click Create Ad to create the ad for the selected product.

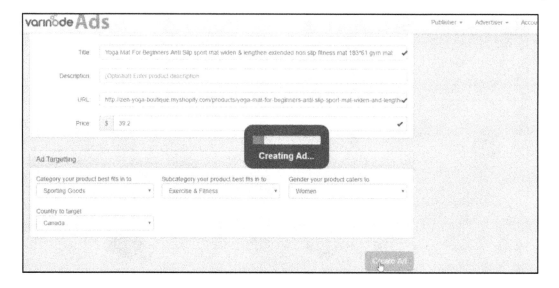

Now you'll see what your chosen ad looks like. The ad will have a simple description and list the category, subcategory, gender, and other information you have provided. Then, for the exchange, since you will advertise a product from someone else, you make your own products available for someone else to advertise and sell.

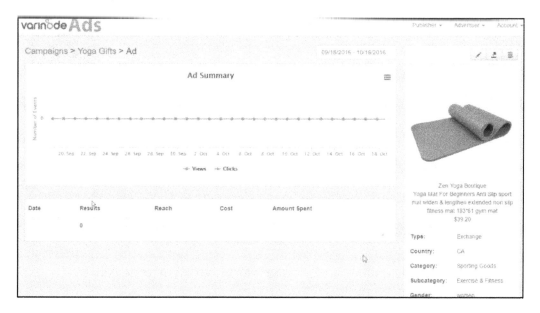

As you add more ads, you'll see them listed by title and how each one is doing.

Your listing of ads will continue to get longer as the number of ads in your exchange program grows.

For more details on how this program works, visit Varinode Ads.

Adding Other Apps

The above apps are just a sampling of the different Shopify apps available to build your business. Just go to the Shopify Apps Store to explore what other apps are available.

CHAPTER 12: CREATING COUPON CODES

Another way to promote your site is by creating coupon codes that enable prospective buyers to get a better deal on one or more products by using that code by a certain date.

You can put your coupon on ads or promote it on special coupon websites, which bring more traffic to your store, helping to increase sales. Using coupon codes is also a way to get backlinks from sites with a high level of traffic, which will increase your own ranking, so you get more organic traffic from search engines.

To create a coupon, choose a coupon code, write a brief coupon description, and indicate the coupon expiration date. Additionally, include your website logo, a description of your website, and the website category for your type of store.

Some Popular Coupon Sites

Some popular coupon sites include these:

RetailMeNot

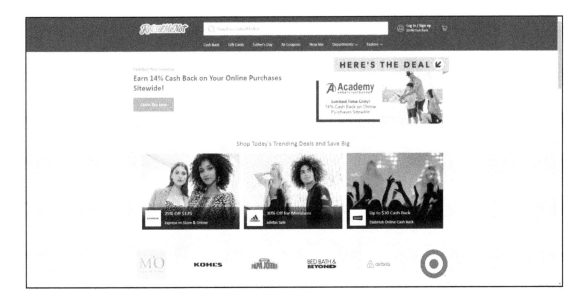

CouponChief

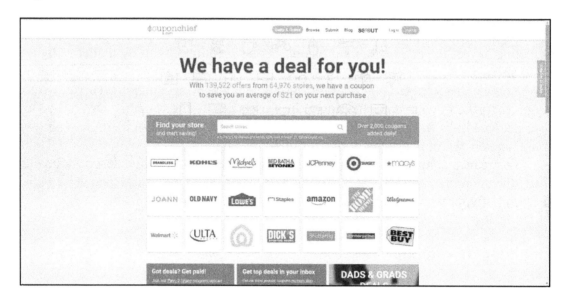

Dealsplus

MightyDeals

Kinja

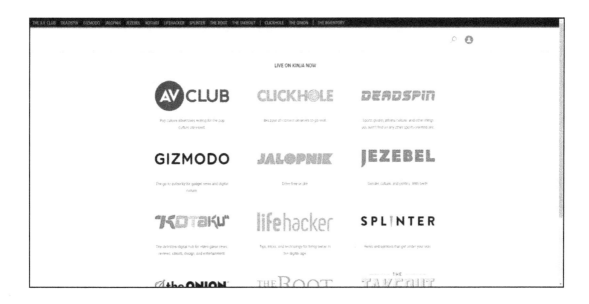

Finding Coupon Creators

A good source of designers to create coupons is Fiverr, a site where individuals from all over the world offer freelance services. These designers can also help with other marketing and promotional materials for your store.

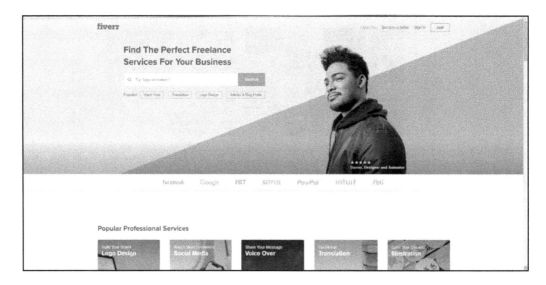

To find coupon creators, search for "submit coupon". You'll get a list of designers who create coupons and you can contact those with the designs you like best. Ask them what they can do for you and their pricing. Some of them will not only create the coupon from information you provide, but they will submit it to up to 50 or 60 of the top coupon sites. Some will design or redesign your Shopify store, too.

You can sort the freelances that turn up in your search by relevance, bestselling coupon creators, or the latest arrivals, who might give you a better price, since they are trying to get established.

You can click on each person's name to see past gigs and reviews.

Here are some examples of reviews.

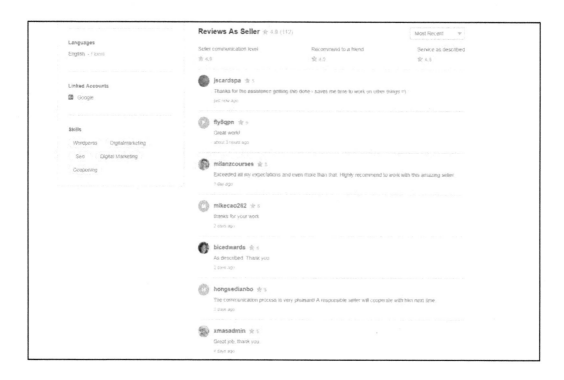

CHAPTER 13: SETTING UP SALES CHANNELS AND ADVERTISING YOUR STORE

Besides setting up sales channels for selling products, consider advertising to build traffic and promote sales. I'll just touch on the sales channels and advertising briefly, since there are books, webinars, courses, blogs, videos, and many other sources of information on how to advertise. And many skilled professionals can handle your marketing, advertising, and promotion for you.

You can add sales channels directly from Shopify. These include the most familiar ones like Facebook, Instagram, Amazon, plus others where you sell your products. Even affiliates might provide a sales channel, if you set up an affiliate program, since they will offer your product for sale in other mostly online venues.

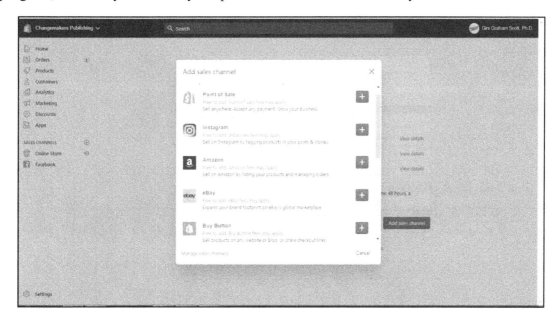

Consider any sales channel a place to advertise. You can place your products for sale directly through that channel, or your ad can direct a prospective buyer to another site to buy. I'll provide an overview here. For more information, go to the instructions, training, or articles available on the website. Or you can buy any number of books, videos, courses, or other materials about advertising on different platforms, most notably Facebook, Instagram, and Amazon.

135

Advertising on Facebook

To advertise on Facebook, create an account or set up a page for your store on an account your already have. Create a daily, weekly, or monthly budget, and Facebook will bill you after you reach your budget limit through click through advertising or at the end of the month for all of your ads.

You can integrate your Facebook advertising directly with your store. Put in the name of your store to connect.

Facebook will then set up your ad account and connect to your pages.

You can specify your campaign objectives, and sometimes, a Facebook staffer will help you set up your target market, budget, and other ad components.

To create your ad, go to the Ad Manager. While you can boost a post for any budget you set, you can more precisely target your ad with the Ad Manager. With a boosted ad, you are just paying for reach - as little as $1 a day to reach the type of people in the categories you select, such as by location, age, and gender. But with an ad set up through Ad Manager, you pay for only the number of clicks you get, regardless of how many people see your ad.

To see how your ads on Facebook are performing, you can create a Facebook Pixel and put that on your Shopify website. It will show you how many people from Facebook are going to your site. While you can install this pixel yourself, a web designer can easily insert this pixel for you.

To start the process, go to the Facebook Pixel link and click "Create Pixel."

Next, give your pixel a name.

After Facebook creates your pixel, install it on your Shopify website yourself or copy the code and send it to your web designer to set up the pixel for you.

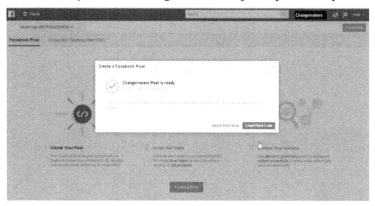

To install a Pixel Code, go to your store and click on preferences.

You'll see an option to set up a Facebook Pixel. Enter the Pixel ID you get, hit save, and you're done.

To get details about the number of visitors to your store and where they are coming from, set up a code you get from Google Analytics on your store site, just as you might set up Google Analytics on any other site.

You can also set up the title of your store in your metadata, which includes the keywords for your site. This metadata helps the search engines know where to find you. If you want a storefront password, enter it here. If adding all of this coding and a password to your site is too technical, your web designer can handle these set ups for you.

Creating a Great Looking Ad

For good results, you need great images, strong ad copy, and the right target audience. For example, since I'm a writer and publisher, I get a lot of ads related to publishing and promotion, even ads to advertise on other platforms, such as an ad to promote my business on Pinterest.

Once you determine your market, make your message short and compelling. Photos and graphics are fine, but advertisers are starting to use videos, which is ideal if your product that can be readily demonstrated, such as in this ad for plush memory foam seats insert that relieves back pain.

If you don't have the time, ability, or interest in creating your ads, look for a pro to set up your advertising.

Testing Out Your Ad and Marketing Campaign

When you start advertising anything -- from a product to a company -- try out different strategies and content to see what works, then double down on that. Start with a small budget -- about $1 to $5 a day or $7 to $35 a week. As something works, you can go up in increments.

Getting feedback from others, especially professionals in your field can help. But you have to see how the marketplace responds, too.

In doing these tests, make changes in different ad elements, such as the photo or video, the headline, and your message. Try pitching your ad to different target markets, too, ands using different sales channels or platforms. Then, keep track of the different campaigns and the results. As in this example below, you can use this kind of format for your Facebook campaigns, as well as your results on different platforms.

	Campaign Name	nt S...	Ends	Refsh...	Cost p...	Purchas...	Add to C...	Cost p...	View Co...	Cost p...
	Funnel 4 - Banner - Fans of Popular Boho sites in...	6	Ongoing	4	$28.17	$262.00	36	$3.13	1,020	$0.11
	Funnel 4 - Banner - Fens of Popular Boho sites in...	74	Ongoing	2	$75.37	$76.70	96	$1.75	2,602	$0.06
	Add to Cart Conversions - Funnel 4 - fans of Popu...		Ongoing	1	$16.95	$16.85	9	$1.88	145	$0.12
	Funnel 1 - Banner - Interested in "Boho Chic"		Ongoing	1	$42.04	$12.95	22	$1.91	1,019	$0.04
	Funnel 5 - Banner w/ Coupon Code		Ongoing	1	$23.60	$43.85	22	$1.07	231	$0.10
	Funnel 3 - Banner w/ Coupon Code - Copy		Ongoing	--	--	$0.00	5	$7.20	200	$0.18
	Funnel 1 - Banner - Interested in "Boho Chic" - Co...		Ongoing	--	--	$0.00	--	--	168	$0.03
	Results from 21 Campaigns	7		9 Total	$56.03 Per Action	$412.35 Total	201 Total	$2.51 Per Action	6,320 Total	$0.08 Per Action

Using E-Mail Marketing

E-mail is another way to promote your business. You can build your email list in various ways. You can get business cards at meetings and trade shows, post ads on social media, and use good keywords, so the website for your store or company is found in a search. Also, having a sample product to give away in return for an email is a common

141

practice. For instance, give away a few chapters from a book in a PDF format if you are publishing books or offer some tips to better health if you have a health product.

It is also possible to buy targeted lists from list brokers. But, before you use it, test the emails and get rid of bounces and incorrect information, like the wrong name associated with that email. Offer recipients an ability to correct their information or unsubscribe from your list and delete any bounces for future mailings.

However you obtain emails, in your mailings to those on the list, send a mixture of free gifts, tips, or special offers, along with a link to a page on a website or in your store where prospective customer can buy.

Mailing Services

A few services for sending out automated and personalized emails to your list include MailChimp, Constant Contact, Get Response, and AWeber. Contact these services directly to learn more about them and decide on the best mailing service for you.

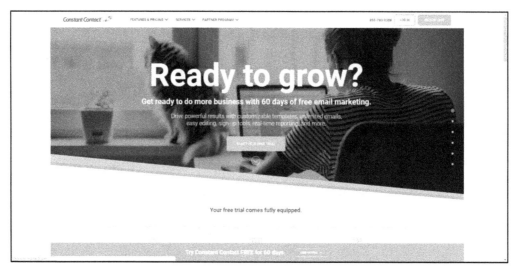

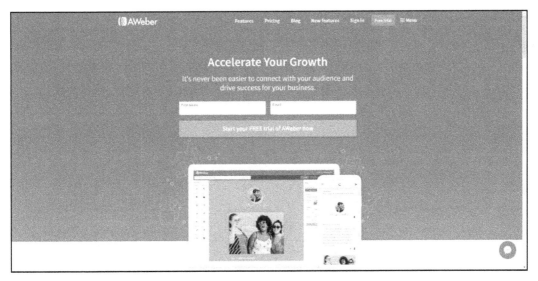

SMTP Mailing Services

Another way to do mailings is through a SMTP mailing service which you can combine with a service that personalizes your message and sends it through your SMTP provider.

Some of the providers I have worked with include SendGrid, SMTP2GO, and SMTP.

Other Places to Sell and Advertise

Other places to post and advertise are Instagram and Pinterest if your product lends itself to product images, people using the product, or photos of subjects in a book. Consider the major demographics of the venue, too. For example, Instagram tends to have a younger audience of teens to young adults in their 20s and 30s, while Pinterest tends to appeal especially to women of 30 and up. Both platforms have been expanding to appeal to a broader audience, though their original core audience remains strong.

After you open an account on these platforms, you'll see postings based on your profile and stated interests. Once you start posting yourself, you can advertise by promoting individual posts, and commonly you will get a notice inviting you to promote each post. Alternatively, you can place a targeted ad. For example, here are my home pages on Instagram and Pinterest.

Besides these major social media sites, you may find other sites that appeal to your audience. To find them, do a Google search. Put in keywords for your product (i.e.: books, jewelry, fashion) and add a word or phrase for what you are looking for, such as "websites", "social media sites," "groups," or "publications," and see what turns up.

As with advertising on the major social media sites, use a limited budget at first and test your results, based on how well different ads perform in getting clicks or conversions to sales.

CHAPTER 14: CREATING DISCOUNT CODES

As an incentive for customers to buy now or within a short time, you can create discount codes to increase sales and reward customers.   These are like coupon codes which offer a price off a particular item, except these codes usually apply a discount on multiple items in your store. The customer just has to indicate the name of that discount to get it. You indicate a start date and can choose an end date or continue the discount without one. Later, you can end a continued discount manually.

To start, go to the Shopify section for Discounts. Then, create a discount.

Give the Discount Code a name and the start date. Indicate an ending date to limit the length of the discount. If there is no end date, enter as such. In addition, note any conditions for the discount, such as reducing the price by a certain number of dollars. Another condition is whether this discount applies to all orders or if the customer has to order a certain amount to qualify to receive it.

Alternatively, instead of a price off discount, you can offer a percentage off discount, such giving the customer 10% off on selected products for a certain time period.

Finally, you'll see where your discount code has been created. Let customers know to apply this, and they'll get the price reduced by the dollars or percentage discount you have set.

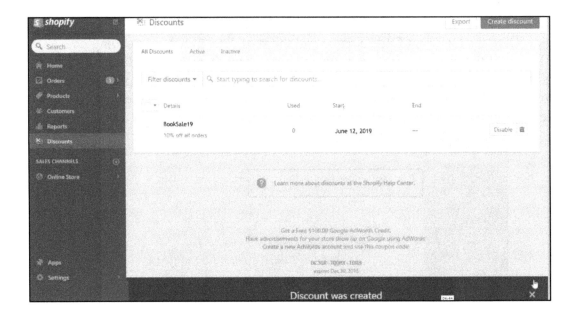

CHAPTER 15: PLANNING YOUR STRATEGY

There you have it -- how to create your store, organize your products into collections, feature selected products, obtain additional products, and promote your store. While you can set up your store on your own website, Shopify gives you a variety of tools for building and promoting your store to help make it a success.

Some prospective customers may find your store by searching Shopify for certain types of products. Beyond that, you have to strategically promote your store so people find it, just as you would promote any company, brand, product line, or service.

Think of these different possibilities for marketing and promotion as having a repertoire of options to choose from, including finding affiliates, creating an email list, using publicity, improving your SEO, advertising your store, and offering coupons and discounts.

To work out your strategy, consider the major market for your product line and the best ways to reach them. Take into consideration your content -- what you say in your communications, how to best present that message with images or video, and where to present it. Then, too, consider your budget -- what you can spend each month for your promotional campaign. Finally, try different approaches to see what works best and double down on that.

To evaluate all of these factors, you might create a spread sheet listing the different options and what message you will promote where. Or bring in a pro that specializes in marketing, advertising, and promotion to help you decide the best strategy for you.

This book provides the basics of how to set up your store and promote it. Then, you have to strategize and choose which approaches to use, based on what will work best for your store.

ABOUT THE AUTHOR

 GINI GRAHAM SCOTT, Ph.D., J.D., is a nationally known writer, consultant, speaker, and seminar leader, specializing in business and work relationships, professional and personal development, social trends, and popular culture. She has published 50 books with major publishers and has worked with dozens of clients on memoirs, self-help, business books, and film scripts. Writing samples are at www.changemakerspublishingandwriting.com.

She is the founder of Changemakers Publishing, featuring books on work, business, psychology, social trends, and self-help. The company has published over 150 print, e-books, and audiobooks. She has licensed several dozen books for foreign sales, including the UK, Russia, Korea, Spain, and Japan.

She has received national media exposure for her books, including appearances on *Good Morning America, Oprah,* and *CNN.*

She is also the writer and executive producer of 10 films in distribution, release, or production. Her most recent films that have been released include *Driver, The New Age of Aging,* and *Infidelity.*

Scott is active in a number of community and business groups, including the Lafayette, Pleasant Hill, and Walnut Creek Chambers of Commerce. She is a graduate of the prestigious Leadership Contra Costa program. She does workshops and seminars on the topics of her books.

She received her Ph.D. from the University of California, Berkeley, and her J.D. from the University of San Francisco Law School. She has received five MAs at Cal State University, East Bay, most recently in Communication.

OTHER AVAILABLE BOOKS ON
INSPIRATION, MOTIVATION, AND SUCCESS

Control Your Life, Control Your Thoughts
Pursue Your Passion
Work It Right
Find True Happiness
The Courage Book
The Gratitude Book
The Anger Book
The Forgiveness Book
The Vision Board Book
Affirming Your Success
Animal Insights
The Animal Experience
20 Rhymes for Your Success
Turn Your Dreams into Reality
The Wisdom of Water: To Your Success
The Wisdom of Water: Insights from Nature for Everyday Life
Mind Power: Picture Your Way to Success in Business
The Empowered Mind: How to Harness the Creative Force Within You

CHANGEMAKERS PUBLISHING
3527 Mt. Diablo Blvd., #273
Lafayette, CA 94549
changemakers@pacbell.net . (925) 385-0608
www.changemakerspublishingandwriting.com

CPSIA information can be obtained
at www.ICGtesting.com
Printed in the USA
BVHW061648160719
553594BV00003B/200/P